THE ROYAL HORTICULTURAL SOCIETY
PRACTICAL GUIDES

LAWNS AND
GROUND COVER

THE ROYAL HORTICULTURAL SOCIETY
PRACTICAL GUIDES

LAWNS AND
GROUND COVER

GEOFF STEBBINGS

DORLING KINDERSLEY
LONDON • NEW YORK • SYDNEY • MOSCOW
www.dk.com

LONDON, NEW YORK, MUNICH, MELBOURNE, DELHI

SERIES EDITOR Pamela Brown
SERIES ART EDITOR Stephen Josland
DESIGNER Anne Thompson

MANAGING EDITOR Louise Abbott
MANAGING ART EDITOR Lee Griffiths

DTP DESIGNER Matthew Greenfield

PRODUCTION Ruth Charlton, Mandy Inness

First published in Great Britain in 1999
Reprinted 2002
by Dorling Kindersley Limited,
80 Strand, London WC2R 0RL

A Penguin Company

A CIP catalogue for this book is available from the British Library.
ISBN 0 7513 47256

Reproduced by Colourscan, Singapore
Printed and bound by Star Standard Industries, Singapore

See our complete catalogue at
www.dk.com

CONTENTS

USING GRASS AND GROUND COVER 7

Why grass makes a perfect garden surface; the alternatives to conventional lawns; when to choose ground cover instead

LAWNS AND LAWN CARE 13

Lawn decisions: high-quality versus hard-wearing; seed versus turf; adding interest with bulbs and specimen trees; how to keep your lawn looking good; alternatives such as herb lawns; making wildflower meadows

PLANTING GROUND COVER 55

How to choose the best plants for cover in your garden, and use them to the best effect

GOOD PLANTS FOR GROUND COVER 64

A selection of shrubs and perennials for easy-care mass plantings

USING GRASS AND GROUND COVER

PLANTS AS GARDEN SURFACES

T HE ADVANTAGES OF COVERING the ground with grass are compelling. It provides a soft surface, ideal for play and relaxation, with a cool, softening appearance, blending well in a rural setting, or enhancing the effect of a green sanctuary in urban gardens. Sown from seed it must be the cheapest of surfaces, and can be maintained to a high standard or with minimal effort. However, it is not always the best solution when choosing plants to cover the ground.

CONSIDERING THE OPTIONS

While grassing over an area sounds simple and attractive, there are alternatives. Is the lawn really going to be used as a working surface? If it is simply a covering for "dead space", perhaps next to a driveway or in a front garden, a creeping mantle of ground

> ## Is a lawn really the best covering for the ground?

cover plants would be easier to maintain and may have the bonus of flowers or fruits. In a pocket-sized garden, a small, decorative lawn could be made of fragrant herbs: more interesting and unusual, and with no need to mow – or to buy and store a mower. The site may not be appropriate: lack of sunlight is a key reason for lawn failure, and alternatives must be sought for shade. Narrow paths might be better made with hard materials: grass will be awkward to cut where plants overhang, and a well-used path will become worn and muddy in winter.

SHADY SURVIVORS
Low maintenance and changing seasonal interest make ground cover an attractive option for areas that need not be walked on; these ajugas thrive in shade where grass would fail.

◀ A RELAXING SPACE *A sunny family garden cries out for a lawn to carpet the "outside room".*

A Brief History of the Lawn

Domestic lawns are a relatively recent component of gardens. Before the invention of the lawn mower, in the 1830s, lawns had to be cut with a scythe or by grazing animals, and were restricted to large estates with sufficient cheap, skilled labour. As mowers developed, lawns became much more commonplace. The first self-propelled mowers can be traced back to the beginning of the 20th century, but the real revolution in cutting grass began in the 1960s with easy-to-use lightweight electric mowers. Maintaining lawns is now easier than ever before, with mowers for every size of lawn, from small push mowers to ride-on machines.

Why Grass?

Grass is the perfect plant for lawns: it grows close to the ground, with its growing points well below the cutting height of a mower. The narrow, tough leaves of grass withstand cutting and continue to lengthen from the base; an important survival

▶ LARGE LAWN
Cheaper to lay than hard surfaces and not so bleak, yet easy to maintain compared to a landscaped garden with beds and borders, this sweep of grass lightly shaded by trees forms an inviting area for play and relaxation.

▼ SMALL LAWN
This small, ornamental lawn has the luminous appeal of a circular pool. A bench and path help to reduce wear and tear on the grass.

▲ FREQUENTLY USED ROUTE
Where lawns are "waisted" by borders and tree canopies, a hard path prevents a muddy trail developing at the bottleneck.

◄ SECLUDED PATHWAY
A grass path forms a perfect, informal route through relaxed cottage-style plantings into woodland at the bottom of a garden.

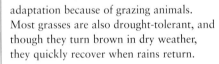

adaptation because of grazing animals. Most grasses are also drought-tolerant, and though they turn brown in dry weather, they quickly recover when rains return.

CASUAL OR PERFECT LAWN?

The very act of cutting grass has a profound effect on the quality of a lawn. Therefore the decision to opt for a fine-leaved sward of verdant perfection or a simple patch of grass is not just about preference, but is also a question of how much time and effort you are willing to put in. Perfect lawns are the result of hard work, from the planning stages to the mowing – twice a week in early summer. Lawns must be fed: grass is a heavy feeder, and lack of fertilizer leads to weak growth. As a result, weeds (or wildflowers), which survive in poorer conditions, will invade the lawn.

Of course, there is nothing wrong with a less than perfect lawn – it would be inappropriate and a waste of time and effort to try to create perfection in a lawn that passes between plantings of shrubs or lies in the shade (and rainshadow) of trees. It is necessary to set realistic targets. The sheer size of a lawn may decide its type, because large areas of grass may become a drain on time and money if maintained to the highest standard.

The traditional compromise is to aim for perfection in a lawn at the front of the house, where it has little wear and will at least impress neighbours and passers-by, but to lower the standard and grow a coarser mixture on the back lawn, where it needs to be able to withstand the rigours of children and pets, ball games, rugs, chairs and other family paraphernalia.

ADDING INTEREST TO LAWNS

Lawns are a rather artificial, sterile environment, but you can add interest in a number of ways. Small trees that do not cast heavy shade add height in an expanse of grass (see p.24), and in time will provide welcome respite from the sun. Spring-flowering bulbs can be planted even in formal lawns (see p.26) to provide some early season colour. If the bulb foliage is left to grow and the grass is not cut until the foliage has started to die down, the bulbs will flourish and the lawn can be kept neat.

A herb lawn (see p.44) is a popular alternative to grass. It is really only possible on a small scale, but suits a semi-formal style well. In an informal setting, a meadow, with long grass where a wide range of wildflowers can flourish, may be more appropriate from an aesthetic viewpoint. It will also attract wildlife, a consideration of growing importance to many gardeners, and it is quite common nowadays for gardens to contain not only a conventional lawn but a small "meadow" area. Cutting twice a year and removing the hay will encourage a rich variety of plants. There are also useful advantages – wildflowers under fruit trees will attract bees to pollinate the crops.

OPTING FOR GROUND COVER

In areas where a lawn is not possible or appropriate, yet a low blanket of weed-smothering ground cover appeals, there are many suitable, spreading perennials and low-growing shrubs to choose from (see Good Plants for Ground Cover, pp.64–77). The wide range of plants available means that effective ground cover is possible in any site, and especially in areas where grass would not survive because the main requirements of light, constant moisture

▶ TAPESTRY OF COLOUR
Thymes and camomile make an eye-catching alternative to grass: the perfect choice for a small centrepiece lawn in a herb or "healing" garden.

▼ SPRING BULBS IN GRASS
Once the chore of initial planting is done, bulbs such as crocuses will naturalize and multiply in grass to bring colour each year, provided that their foliage is not mown down too soon.

and fertile, well-drained soil are not met. Most ground cover plants gain their reputation for usefulness because they are natural survivors and spreaders in adverse conditions: deep shade, for example, or poor, waterlogged soil, where grass would quickly lose the battle to moss. Sadly, many ground cover plants are thought of as utilitarian and dull, but some are beautiful, and even the most ordinary plant will gain impact from being planted *en masse*.

Even a rather dull plant gains impact when planted *en masse*

Ground cover plants will not tolerate being trodden on, however, and if access is needed, you will need to lay a hard path through the planting. If a clearly defined route is not required, consider a more informal combination of low-growing plants with gravel in sun, or with chipped bark in shade; a better option than poor grass.

▲ PACHYSANDRA AS GROUND COVER
This is a classic ground cover choice: low-growing, neat in habit, and glossy and green in leaf all the year round.

▼ CLOVER AND BUTTERCUP MEADOW
A wildflower habitat gives plants that might be considered weeds in conventional borders a place to flourish and benefit wildlife.

LAWNS AND LAWN CARE

PLANNING CONSIDERATIONS

WHETHER FORMAL, with precise edges and flanked by regimented bedding, or informal, dotted with bulbs, made from fragrant herbs, or left to grow long with wildflowers among the grass, lawns remain an important part of most gardens. While they are often sown or laid without much thought, they still form the largest part of most gardens. This is probably because they are the cheapest way to cover large areas of ground – the ultimate ground cover.

HOW GRASS GROWS

Unlike broad-leaved garden plants, the growing points of grass are only just above soil surface, not at shoot tips. This is why constant cutting reinvigorates grass, whereas it would quickly exhaust other plants. Grass spreads in one of two ways, either forming ever-widening clumps, or spreading underground to send up new shoots from creeping (rhizomatous) roots.

CLUMPING GRASS
The clumps broaden and mesh together to form a lawn.

CREEPING GRASS
The plant sends up shoots to colonize bare soil around it.

A QUESTION OF SCALE
The lawn as familiar green oasis in a town garden (left); remember that however small the lawn, you will still need a mower and somewhere to store it. In a rural setting, this meadow style (right) looks perfect and requires far less maintenance.

If your lawn is exposed to heavy wear, it should be made from creeping grasses, such as ryegrasses (*see p.19 for details of seed mixtures*), which, although they will never look perfect, quickly recover from damage. The finest and brightest lawns, however, are composed of tufted grasses, such as the fescues and bents, which have narrow, needle-like leaves and can be mown very short. These do not recover well from wear or from drought, and can be more prone to disease in adverse conditions.

SOWING OR TURFING?

The choice of seed or turf is a complex one (*see opposite*) but, generally speaking, if you want a specialist lawn you are unlikely to find it in the form of turf. Turf can be

▲ SWEEPING CURVES
The simpler the shape of your lawn, the easier mowing will be, and the shorter the perimeter, the easier it will be to maintain a perfect edge.

▼ WEAR AND TEAR
Grass is the perfect soft surface for play, but only coarse, creeping grasses can withstand the constant patter of tiny feet, so choose turf or an appropriate "family lawn" seed mixture.

> You are unlikely to find a specialist lawn in the form of turf

cheap, but you should always see it before you buy. Avoid meadow turf, even if it is sprayed, because it will never be as good as cultivated, seeded turf. For the initial

savings you make on meadow turf, you will face years of frustrating work.

PLANNING AND PREPARATION

If you are planning a new lawn, cultivate the proposed area for as long as possible before you want to sow seed or lay turf, to let the soil settle and to remove perennial weeds. Allow for detours around problem areas in deep shade, or waterlogged areas.

FINE FORMALITY
This fine, closely cut lawn reflects the neatly trimmed box edging that surrounds it.

(Wet soil can sometimes, but not always, be improved with drainage; a consultation with a garden designer or landscaper can be useful.) The next step is to level the ground (*see overleaf*), after which sowing (in the right season) or turfing can begin.

TURF OR SEED?

ADVANTAGES OF TURF

• **Quick results** – it quickly looks established, whereas a sown lawn looks sparse for weeks and cannot be used in its first season.
• **Few problems** with diseases and weeds in the soil, provided that good-quality turf is purchased – always inspect it before you buy.
• **No problems** with preventing dogs, cats and birds scratching or pecking at the sown surface.
• **Soil requires** less thorough preparation – a fine tilth is not needed.
• **Can be laid** in autumn and winter, or at any time except during hot, dry weather.
• **Lawn edges** are clearly defined.
• **Bare patches** can be replaced with new turves as easily as laying a new carpet tile, although matching turf can be a problem.

ADVANTAGES OF SEED

• **Choice of grass species** is usually greater than with turf.
• **Requires less heavy,** physical work than lifting and laying turves.
• **No transport** problems.
• **Seed can be stored** without harm until it is convenient for you to sow, whereas turf must be laid as soon as it is delivered.
• **Economical**
• **Choice of seed mixtures** to suit both lawn type and site.
• **Less chance of weeds** than with standard turf, as long as soil is thoroughly prepared.
• **Bare patches** can be over-sown with the same seed mixture, which will grow to blend in seamlessly with the rest of the lawn.

Preparing the Ground

ONE KEY TO A SUCCESSFUL LAWN is thorough soil preparation. This includes removing all perennial weeds (*see p.58*) and, if sowing seed, annual weed seeds. The soil must then be levelled if necessary, raked, cleared of detritus, firmed and fertilized before seed can be sown or turf laid. The site may also have to be drained or the soil augmented with organic matter.

Using Levelling Tools

To level accurately you need wooden pegs of similar length, a long wooden plank, a spirit level and a hammer. Mark each peg 5cm from the top end. On a spot at the desired level, knock in the first peg down to the mark. Then knock in all the others and adjust until their tops are all level with the first one.

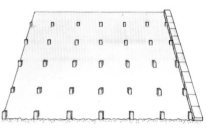

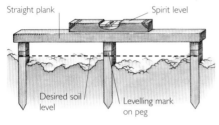

Straight plank   Spirit level

Desired soil level
Levelling mark on peg

LEVELLING METHODS
Set out marker pegs in a grid (above) then use the plank and spirit level across them (left) to make sure they align in every direction, adjusting the height of the pegs as necessary. Rake and firm the soil to the marks; fill in hollows with more topsoil.

CREATING A SLOPE▶
For a gentle slope, mark the pegs with lines at increasing distances from the top. Knock the pegs in across the site so that the tops are level; raking the soil to the marks gives a gradient.

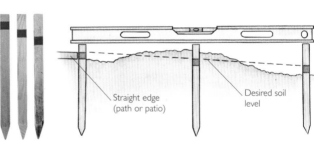

Straight edge (path or patio)
Desired soil level

Laying a Simple Drain

In small areas, install a soakaway drain (*right*) at the lowest point, but well away from any house walls. A herringbone pattern of drains running into the lowest area is needed for large areas. Excavate a trench and line the base with rubble and coarse gravel. If the problem is severe, fill the base of the trench with gravel, lay clay pipe or perforated tubes on top, cover with coarser material and refill with soil.

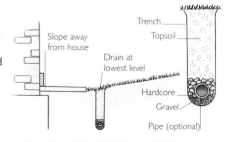

Slope away from house

Drain at lowest level

Trench
Topsoil

Hardcore
Gravel
Pipe (optional)

Creating a Level Base

In gardens that have only minor undulations and deep topsoil, the site may be roughly levelled by raking soil from the high spots to fill the hollows, firming at intervals. Although it is not essential for the ground to be precisely level, awkward bumps and hollows may cause problems when mowing. In some instances, such as a meadow or rough grass, levelling by eye may be sufficient. However, if a perfectly level surface is required, such as for a formal lawn, a more accurate method such as the one shown here should be used. After the first levelling, give the soil time to settle and tread the site evenly to firm it and eliminate soft spots, filling these and levelling again if necessary.

1 **Firm the site** well with a rake or by trampling it. Insert a row of marker pegs (*see* Using Levelling Tools, *opposite*) on the site edge.

2 **Add a second,** parallel row of pegs about 1m from the first row. Place a spirit level on top to check that they are level with the previous row. Adjust the pegs as necessary.

3 **Repeat the process** to create a grid of pegs. Rake the soil to the top of the marks on the pegs, adding topsoil to fill any hollows. Once the ground is level, remove the pegs.

Preparing the Soil Surface

1 **Firm the soil surface** by treading it evenly or by tamping it with the back of a rake. Repeat the process until the entire site is firmed well.

2 **Rake the soil** to a fine tilth and leave for 10–20 days so any weeds may germinate. Apply a weedkiller and, after 2–3 days, rake off the weeds.

3 **Apply a base dressing** of a compound granular or micro-granular fertilizer and lightly rake in. Leave for a few days before turfing or seeding.

SEEDING A LAWN

W HEN SOWING A LAWN, it is especially important first to leave the prepared ground for 10–20 days so that annual weed seeds brought to the surface will germinate and can be lightly hoed or sprayed off. This "stale seedbed" technique is also very useful when planting out massed bedding or sowing annuals in drifts.

SOWING GRASS SEED

Sowing (*below*) is a simple business compared with choosing from the wide range of grass seed and mixtures available. Avoid buying an unspecified mix; instead, choose one that suits your purpose. Mixtures containing ryegrass (which recovers well from overuse) were once considered inferior, even for utility lawns destined for a lot of wear, but modern ryegrasses have fine leaves and an attractive appearance. Fine-leaved grasses can be cut more closely than coarser types. The special mixtures for light shade contain meadow grasses that must not be cut too closely.

MARKING OUT SMALL AREAS
If seeding small areas, you can mark out measured square metres with pots or sticks and scatter seed between them.

MAKING A GRID
Use metre-long canes to divide up the site. Weigh out each portion of seed, scattering half up-and-down and half side-to-side.

SEEDING WITH A SPREADER
Sow half the seed in one direction and half at right angles to it. For a defined edge, lay down plastic and push the machine just over it.

SEEDING CURVED AREAS

To mark out curved edges, use a pair of sticks and a piece of string to draw a line. Use this line as a guide for sowing. When seeding a lawn that is to be enclosed by beds, sow a little beyond the area and trim back the grass later, again using sticks and a line.

MARKING CURVES
Insert one stick in the ground and use the other to trace the line.

Covering and Protecting the Seed

2 The new grass seedlings should take 7–14 days to emerge. Once the grass is about 5cm high, cut it to a height of 2.5cm with a rotary mower.

KEEPING BIRDS OFF SEED

- Scare birds away from the sown area using strips of foil suspended from sticks or a humming line set above the soil.
- Use seed that is treated with a repellent, which tastes unpleasant but does not harm the birds.
- Cover small areas with fine chicken wire.
- Cover spring-sown lawns with fleece.
- Try children's plastic windmills to scare off some birds.
- Attract birds to another part of the garden by providing them with food there.

1 **After sowing,** lightly rake over the soil surface to cover the seed. If conditions are dry, water the site regularly to keep the soil moist and encourage the seeds to germinate.

SOWING TIMES AND RATES

WHEN TO SOW

The best times to sow are mid-spring or early autumn when the soil is moist, but not wet.
- **Spring sowing** has the disadvantage that the seedlings require constant watering in dry weather until the lawn is established. Also, the lawn will not be ready to walk on for many months, by which time summer may be over.
- **Autumn-sown** lawns will withstand light wear the following summer. Sow on a dry, windless day to avoid the seed blowing away.

SOWING TIPS

- **Sowing seed** too thickly has no advantage, unless you have a severe problem with birds.
- **To avoid** sowing unevenly, always mark out the site into sections, then measure out and sow seed for each section. Do not be tempted to broadcast the seed over a large area.
- **Weigh out** an average 25–40g of seed, or the recommended rate for the species (*see right*), for each square metre of lawn. Alternatively, weigh out a larger quantity and divide it by eye into the correct number of portions.

SOWING RATES

- **Mixtures with fescues and bents**
Fine-leaved grasses for quality lawns and close mowing: 25–30g/sq m
- **Mixtures with ryegrass and other grasses**
Coarser grasses for utility lawns: 35–40g/sq m
- **Single species**
Single species are generally warm-climate grasses. They go brown at temperatures below 10°C and do not mix well with other species, but grow faster in warm climates.
Bents (*Agrostis*) 8–10g/sq m
Carpet grass (*Axonopus*) 8–12g/sq m
Common Bermuda grass (*Cynodon dactylon*) 5–8g/sq m
Centipede grass (*Eremochloa ophiuroides*) 1.5–2.5g/sq m
Red fescue (*Festuca rubra* var. *rubra*) 15–25g/sq m
Perennial ryegrass (*Lolium perenne*) 20–40g/sq m
Bahia grass (*Paspalum notatum*) 30-40g/sq m
Smooth-stalked meadow grass/Kentucky blue grass (*Poa pratensis*) 10–15g/sq m

TURFING A LAWN

THE ADVANTAGE THAT TURF HAS over sowing seed is that the effect is almost instant. But the laid turf must be allowed to become established before it can be walked on, and must be kept moist to prevent the turves shrinking and browning at the edges. Turf can be laid at almost any time of the year, but best times are autumn or early spring. Avoid laying in rain or frosty weather. Turf laid in summer can be difficult to keep moist, although it will establish quickly.

BUYING AND STORING TURF

Planning is the secret of successfully laying turf. In addition to calculating the area of turf needed (and allowing an extra 5% for wastage), you need to coordinate the delivery of the turf with your soil preparation, and have the time to lay it. Try to view the turf before you buy it to ensure its quality. Good, seeded turf is usually cut into larger turves that are rolled rather than folded like traditional turf. If you cannot lay them when they arrive (you need dry weather), the turves can be left for up to three days. If stored for longer, they will start to turn yellow, so unroll them (*right*) and keep them watered until you are ready to lay them.

LEFTOVER TURF

It is important to buy more than enough turf so that the entire lawn can be completed from a single, consistent batch. Leftovers can be put to good use; stacked upside-down out of the way, they will eventually break down into a fine soil ideal for lawn top-dressing (*see p.31*).

▶ KEEPING TURF FRESH
If you are not ready to lay turves when they arrive, unroll them onto plastic sheeting or soil, and water well every day to keep moist.

PLUGS AND SPRIGS

These small pieces of spreading grasses are used to establish lawns in warm climates. It is normal to use just one type of grass to prevent a "blotchy" appearance. The grasses tolerate extreme conditions, but do not form as fine a sward as cool-climate grasses. Soil must be prepared in advance since, like turf, plugs or sprigs are living plant material that cannot be stored for any period of time. Plugs (tufts of rhizomatous grass) are planted in individual holes; new shoots grow from the joints, quickly knitting together. Sprigs (sections of root) are scattered evenly over the surface, covered with a thin layer of soil, then watered in well.

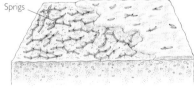

Plugs

Sprigs

LAYING THE TURF

1 **Lay the first** row of turves along a straight edge, such as a path. Place each new turf flush against its neighbour.

2 **Place a plank** on the first row of turves. Use this to kneel on. Then lay the next row with the turf joints staggered, as in a brick wall. Proceed in exactly the same way for the rest of the lawn. Avoid walking on the bare soil. Use any small pieces of turf in the centre of the lawn.

SETTLING IN TURF

1 **Tamp down** each piece with the back of a rake to eliminate air pockets and to ensure good root contact with the soil. Alternatively, roll the lawn with a light roller.

2 **Apply a light** top-dressing of sieved, sandy loam and brush this in, filling any gaps between the turves. Give the new lawn a good soak and keep it moist in dry weather.

TRIMMING THE TURF EDGE

STRAIGHT EDGE
Stretch a taut string along the required line and position a plank against it. Standing on the plank, cut along the line with a lawn edger to trim it.

CURVED EDGE
Use string attached to a stake and a funnel of fine, dry sand to measure out an arc, or lay down a hose or a rope and secure it with wire hoops.

TURFING TIPS
• Start laying the turf at the part of the lawn closest to the stored turves.
• Work from a plank to avoid compacting the turf.
• Integrate small pieces of turf into the centre of the lawn, not at the edge, where they may dry and shrink.
• Stagger the turf joints, as for bricks in a wall.
• Lay the turf beyond the desired shape and trim later.
• Make the first cut at maximum mower height.

EDGES AND PATHS

THE EDGE OF A LAWN CAN BE ONE of its most important features. Even if the grass is not perfect, a neat edge gives the impression that the lawn and the surrounding borders are well cared for. Main routes across the turf can quickly become worn, especially in wet weather and in winter. Frosted turf should not be walked on. A path across the lawn may not only be practical, but can also be a design feature that leads the eye to another part of the garden.

BREAKING INTO A LAWN
When the lawn edge has an intricate shape, avoid placing tall plants in borders and high structures close to the edges. Here a step is surrounded by an area of brick paving which allows the mower to get right up to the edge of the grass, eliminating the need to trim it separately. It also forms an "apron" that avoids grass wear at the base of the step.

STEPPING STONES

Stepping stones in grass provide a simple way to prevent wear. Use groups of brick or paving slabs, set on beds of sand, or use riven stone for a less formal effect. Slabs of tree trunk can also be set into the grass in shady areas, but they can become slippery if wet and do not last so long.

▶ USEFUL AND DECORATIVE
This line of stepping stones helps to reduce grass wear in an area that is regularly walked on. It also has a softer line than a solid path and leads the eye to the secluded area beyond.

HOW TO LAY STEPPING STONES

Lay the slabs on the grass in their proposed places and leave for several days, walking over them now and then to ensure that they form a sensible route and are at the correct spacing. When you are satisfied with the result, cut round each slab with a lawn edger or spade, lift the slab, and remove the turf. Add sand to the hole, level it, and drop in the slab, or slide it down over a broom handle laid across the hole to avoid trapping your fingers.

HARD AND SOFT EDGING

A neat edge, whether cut with an edging iron, or fitted with an edging strip, is easier to cut after mowing. Although a simple, cut lawn edge is the most common type of edging, using an edging strip, or surrounding the area with bricks or paving, makes cutting the edges simpler. Hard edging also stops plants overhanging the grass and causing dead patches in summer. The edging strip can be narrow and functional, or wide to link the edge to a patio or garden feature. Wide slabs can be decorated with pots to add colour if the border is dull at any time. In time, lawns that are cut with an edging iron each spring can lose their shape and get smaller, a problem with curved and circular lawns.

HARD EDGING
A combination of narrow stone pavers and terracotta edging tiles are practical and visually pleasing.

SOFT EDGING
Without an edging strip, plants must be staked to prevent them from sprawling across the lawn.

MOWING STRIPS AND EDGES

A "mowing strip" around the lawn makes mowing and edging easier and gives a neat effect. A strip of brick edging laid at or just below the height of the soil eliminates the need to trim the edge, because the mower can glide straight over it without damage.

An invisible, sunken holding strip, usually available as corrugated plastic or wood (which will not last as long), is a good choice for traditional beds in grass or where the grass joins gravel or loose mulches that make edge-cutting difficult.

◀ MOWING STRIP
A traditional "gutter" of bricks laid on mortar or sand between the flower bed and the edge of the lawn prevents the plants from shading the grass and makes mowing and edging easier.

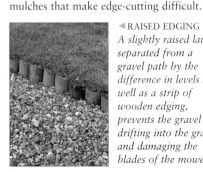

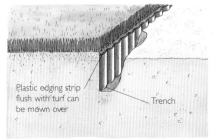

◀ RAISED EDGING
A slightly raised lawn, separated from a gravel path by the difference in levels as well as a strip of wooden edging, prevents the gravel drifting into the grass and damaging the blades of the mower.

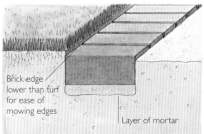

Brick edge lower than turf for ease of mowing edges

Layer of mortar

Plastic edging strip flush with turf can be mown over

Trench

TREES IN LAWNS

THERE IS OFTEN LIMITED ROOM for trees in gardens, and the shade they cast is too deep for most beds and borders. An alternative is to site trees in lawns. Deep-rooting, deciduous trees are best; avoid dense, spreading evergreens that will cast heavy shade. Grass should be kept away from the tree roots in the early years, so it need not compete for nutrients and water.

SUITABLE TREES

An advantage of growing a tree in a lawn is that, freed from the competition of any neighbouring plants, the tree can achieve its natural shape and size, which can be shown off to perfection. Choose a small tree unless the size of your garden is extensive, and use something with a striking shape such as a narrowly upright (fastigiate) or weeping tree.

DISTINCTIVE OUTLINE
A specimen tree will look most striking if it is planted against the uncluttered background of a lawn. Simplicity is often most effective and a single tree with an attractive, airy branch structure, like this flowering cherry, can be beautiful. The lower branches may need to be removed to reduce shade on the grass and allow mowing in summer, and to show off spring-flowering bulbs that can be naturalized beneath once the tree is mature.

PLANTING A TREE IN A LAWN

1 Dig a large hole and hammer in a low stake, off-centre and to the windward side in exposed areas.

2 Lay the tree on its side and slide it out of its pot. Tease out the roots carefully and remove any weeds.

3 Hold the tree next to the stake and spread the roots. Lay a cane across the hole to check the planting depth.

5 Spread a thick layer of organic mulch around the tree to keep the soil moist and to hinder growth of annual weeds. Do not let the mulch touch the tree trunk.

GOOD TREES FOR LAWNS

Acer davidii
Arbutus × andrachnoides ♥
Calocedrus decurrens ♥
Cornus florida
Corylus colurna ♥
Fraxinus excelsior 'Pendula' ♥
Magnolia × soulangeana
Malus tschonoskii ♥
Parrotia persica ♥
Prunus 'Spire' ♥
Prunus × subhirtella 'Autumnalis' ♥
Pyrus salicifolia 'Pendula' ♥
Quercus robur f. *fastigiata*
Salix caprea 'Kilmarnock' ♥
Sophora japonica ♥
Sorbus × thuringiaca 'Fastigiata'

4 Adjust the planting depth by adding or removing soil. Backfill with more soil mixed with organic matter, firm around the tree by treading, fork over the soil, and water.

PLANTING BULBS UNDER TREES

Many small bulbs thrive under deciduous trees, especially woodland plants such as colchicums (autumn crocus) and cyclamen. A mulch of leaf mould around the tree will suit them well. In the early stages, it is easy to plant bulbs in the circle of soil around the tree, but for a more natural effect you could extend the planting into the surrounding grass (*see p.77*).

COLCHICUMS IN FLOWER UNDER A TREE

1 Make a hole deep enough to plant each bulb (or, as here, a cyclamen corm), with any roots spread out.

2 Plant so the bulb or corm lies with its upper surface just visible at soil level. Fill in around the roots with soil.

3 Firm the surrounding soil gently, leaving the growing point exposed. Apply a light mulch of leaf mould.

BULBS IN GRASS

Some bulbs, such as tulips, usually look best in formal surroundings, but daffodils can excel themselves when they are released from borders and planted in grass. Smaller blooms tend to look more natural. Plant one or two types only: mixtures will flower sporadically, instead of giving a mass display. Bear in mind that daffodil flowers face away from the shade, into the light, and this may affect where they are planted. After flowering, the fading leaves should not be cut down too soon, or tied up (*see below*).

SPRING CHARM
To achieve a naturalistic effect, scatter the bulbs randomly (inset) then plant them where they fall, at least their own width apart.

PLANTING LARGE BULBS IN GRASS

1 **Clean the bulbs.** For each bulb, use a bulb planter to remove a core of turf and soil to a depth of 12–15cm.

2 **Wearing gloves,** place a pinch of bone meal and a little soil into each hole. Put in a bulb, growing point upward.

3 **Break up** the underside of the soil core and cover the bulb with it. Then replace the remains of the core on top.

4 **Replace** the lid of turf, and firm it gently to protect the growing point. Fill in gaps in the turf with more soil.

CUTTING DOWN BULB FOLIAGE

The leaves of bulbs should be allowed to grow on for about six weeks after they have flowered. Then, the grass can be cut and the planted patches will be indistinguishable in summer. If the grass has grown too long to cut with your mower, cut small areas with shears (*right*) or a line trimmer first, taking care not to damage the grass.

PLANTING SMALL BULBS IN GRASS

The easiest way to plant large quantities of bulbs is to lift the turf and plant in groups. This causes less damage to the grass than making individual holes and replacing small turf plugs, which are liable to dry out. Alternatively, insert a fork into the soil and rock it backwards and forwards to make holes into which small bulbs can be pushed. For the best effect, plant large drifts by grouping lifted areas of turf.

1 **Using a half-moon** edger (or spade), cut an "H" shape in the turf. Cut to the full depth of the half-moon blade to make sure that it penetrates to the soil below.

2 **Undercut the turf** and carefully fold back the flaps to expose the area of bare soil beneath. Handle the turf gently, taking care not to crack or tear it unduly.

3 **Using a hand fork,** loosen the compacted soil beneath the turf to a depth of at least 7cm, mixing in a little bone meal at a rate of approximately 15g/sq m.

4 **Press the bulbs** (*here crocuses*) gently into the soil, taking care not to damage their growing points. Space the bulbs randomly but keep them at least 2.5cm apart.

5 **Score the underneath** of the turf with the hand fork to loosen the soil, so that the bulbs will be able to penetrate the turf easily. Roll back the turf flaps and firm them down.

GOOD BULBS FOR GRASS

Allium (small types such as *A. moly* ♥)
Anemone apennina ♥, *A. blanda* ♥
Camassia leichtlinii ♥
Chionodoxa forbesii
Colchicum autumnale, C. speciosum ♥
Crocus biflorus, C. chrysanthus, C. Dutch Hybrids, *C. flavus, C. nudiflorus*
Galanthus caucasicus ♥, *G. nivalis* ♥
Leucojum aestivum, L. vernum ♥ (snowflake)
Narcissus Miniature hybrids, *N. cyclamineus* ♥
Tulipa sprengeri ♥

LOOKING AFTER YOUR LAWN

LIKE ANY OTHER PLANT IN THE GARDEN, how well grass grows after planting will depend on the care it receives. Dead grass, known as thatch, must be regularly removed (*see p.30*) as it forms a layer at the soil surface which can choke out new growth. Regular mowing (*see p.32*) is essential to keep a lawn neat, but every time clippings are removed, the turf is impoverished. Feeding is needed if grass is to flourish and form a thick lawn that will exclude weeds.

THE BENEFITS OF FEEDING

Grass flourishes when there are high levels of nutrients; unfed lawns are more prone to disease, are often patchy, and have moss and weeds, which dominate in poorer soil. Feeding will not necessarily make the grass grow so much faster that it needs more frequent mowing, but there may be more in the grass box each time. Use a supplementary "lawn tonic", if you wish, to keep fine lawns looking good all season.

WHAT IS LAWN FOOD?

Lawn feeds differ from general-purpose fertilizers; they are especially formulated to provide all the essential nutrients that grass requires for good root and leaf growth. Most lawn foods are applied (*see opposite*) in granular form, often in combination with chemicals to control moss and other lawn weeds – "feed-and-weed" mixtures.

▶ SUMMER TONIC
In summer, soluble lawn tonics can be applied by hose or watering-can while the soil is moist. These tonics are high in nitrogen and give a quick greening effect. Their action is short-lived and applications must be repeated at regular intervals. Because they are applied diluted in water they rarely cause scorching of the turf.

◀ BULBS IN GRASS
It may not be economical to feed large areas of lawn every year where a high-quality turf is not required, but an extra feed will be necessary to keep bulbs growing strongly and flowering freely. Apply this in early spring before the bulbs flower so that they can gain the full benefit of the fertilizer before the grass begins to grow away strongly.

When to Water?

It is not always possible to water during dry summer spells, but do not despair; grass usually fully recovers when rain moistens the soil, no matter how dead it appears. However, new lawns and fine lawns do need watering. Water in the evening, so less will evaporate, once a week. Watering lightly is bad for the lawn: give no less than 1cm, measured by placing jars or saucers on the lawn surface.

INSUFFICIENT WATER TO BENEFIT GRASS

GOOD PENETRATION OF WATER IN TURF

Applying Lawn Feed

The fertilizer formulations that lawns need vary at different times of the year. In spring, more nitrogen is needed to replace what has leached from the soil in winter and to "green up" the lawn. A fertilizer with more potassium is given in late summer which toughens the grass ready for winter. Lawn fertilizers are usually applied as granules or powder, and these release nutrients over a period of several weeks or more. They should be applied when the grass is in growth, when the soil is moist and before rain is forecast, so that the fertilizer will be washed into the soil. Fertilizers must be applied evenly, by hand (*below*) or on larger lawns using a spreader (*right*). Grass will be scorched by overlapping, double applications of fertilizer, especially if a feed-and-weed mixture is being used; many products are brightly coloured to help avoid this. Always apply half the feed working up and down the area, and half from side to side, to get even coverage. Cut off the flow of fertilizer at each turn.

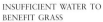

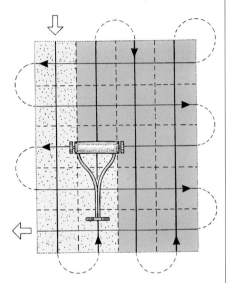

USING A SPREADER
Apply half the feed one way, and half the other (above) *to reduce the risk of scorch* (left).

◄ FEEDING BY HAND
Small lawns can be fed by measuring the fertilizer into portions and dividing the lawn into measured squares. Scatter half the feed in one direction and the remainder at right-angles to achieve an even spread.

Hopper releases fertilizer evenly

FERTILIZER SPREADER

LAWN JOBS FOR AUTUMN

IN ADDITION TO FEEDING, GRASS NEEDS regular care to keep it healthy and vigorous. The main obstacles to grass growth are choking at soil level, caused by accumulation of dead grass, or thatch, and compaction of the soil from constant wear. Both problems, of choking and compaction, can be overcome by scarifying and aeration – two tasks for early autumn. It is not always necessary to aerate the entire lawn, but concentrate on areas that are used as paths.

SCARIFYING

Scarifying involves raking vigorously with a spring-tined or sharp-toothed rake, pushing it well down to pull out the dead grass or moss and break stems of creeping grasses. This clears out dead matter and allows air to reach the live grass, which then grows to fill the spaces. Scarify two weeks after using a moss-killer to remove the dead moss.

SCARIFYING RAKE
This cuts deeply into thatch and even into the turf itself. Its rigid, metal tines are usually flat with sharp points.

SCARIFYING WITH AN ORDINARY RAKE
Pull a spring-tined rake vigorously across the lawn to remove any thatch and dead moss. Ensure that the tines of the rake are pushed well down into the soil surface.

REMOVING FALLEN LEAVES

Fallen leaves in autumn may look lovely on a lawn, but if left they shade the grass and slow its growth. A thick layer will exclude air and encourage disease. Leaves on the surface also attract worms which pull the leaves into the soil. Although invaluable in other parts of a garden, in a lawn a great deal of worm activity results in a multitude of casts *(see p.38)* which, if flattened by mowers or treading, smother the grass. Rake or sweep up the leaves and add them to the compost heap or a leaf mould bin.

LEAF SWEEPING
A leaf sweeper (below) saves the effort of raking or brushing away dead leaves (left). Rotating brushes gather up the leaves and collect them in a large bag.

LEAF MOULD
This is a good soil conditioner and mulch. Make it up in a separate heap from compost.

Aerating the Grass

Aerating is a method of alleviating soil compaction by making deep, narrow holes in the turf. The simplest way is to force a digging fork into the soil at 15cm intervals across the entire grassed area. It is quicker, however, to use a rotary aerator, especially when working on large lawns. On heavy soils, use a hollow-tine aerator that cuts out soil plugs. This will improve surface drainage. The plugs should be removed and composted. Then a prepared top-dressing of gritty compost is swept into the turf.

HOLLOW-TINING
Use a purpose-designed tool, working methodically across the lawn, to lift out cores of grass and soil 0.5–2cm wide. Brush these from the turf.

SPIKING
For small lawns, spiking using a garden fork is adequate; insert the fork straight, then rock it to and fro slightly to let more air into the soil.

SLITTING
Slitting must be done with a special machine which may be available to hire; the expense can be worth the amount of labour saved on large lawns.

Top-dressing after Aerating

Top-dressings are used to fill holes left by aeration, to keep the passages open and to feed the grass and stimulate growth, or to fill in and level small hollows in the lawn surface. They usually consist of a mixture of sand, peat substitute and loam, but the loam must be sieved to prevent stones being spread over the lawn surface and causing problems with mowing. The best time of year to apply a top-dressing is in early autumn. If your lawn is in good condition, you may not need to top-dress every year.

6 parts medium-fine sand
3 parts sieved soil
1 part peat

TOP-DRESSING MIX
Prepare the top dressing by mixing medium-fine sand with clean topsoil and either peat substitute, peat or leaf mould. Pass the mixture through a 5mm mesh sieve to pick out any stones.

APPLYING A TOP-DRESSING
For a large lawn, it is most convenient to hire a spreader to top-dress. Weigh out the correct amount of top-dressing for the lawn area (at a rate of about 3kg/sq m) and apply it on a dry day.

TOP-DRESSING SMALL AREAS
The top dressing may be applied by hand for small areas; spread it evenly over the grass using a shovel or spade. Use a stiff brush to even out any excess and to work it into the grass.

MOWING

MOWING IS THE SINGLE MOST important method of maintaining a lawn in good condition. The ideal is to mow often but not to take off too much grass each time. This encourages the grass to give a denser cover and inhibits weeds. Irregular mowing or cutting the grass too low encourages weeds and moss, and weakens the grass. Always use a grass box or clippings will collect at soil level and produce a thatch, which will choke the grass.

WHICH MOWER?

For small lawns an electric mower is quiet and convenient, but a petrol mower is more practical for large areas where a lead can be awkward. Cylinder mowers give the grass attractive stripes but they must be correctly adjusted or they will tear the grass instead of cutting. Rotary mowers are easy to use but, unless they have a back-roller, they will not give good stripes. Their blades slash the grass but are suitable for all but the finest lawns. Hover mowers are useful for sloping lawns and banks.

▶ METHODS OF CUTTING
Rotary mowers cut the grass by slashing it at high speed. Even if blunted, the blades will cut the grass, though the cut tips will turn brown and look unsightly. A cylinder mower cuts the grass like a series of sharp scissors and is kinder to the grass leaves, but if not properly adjusted and kept sharp can cut poorly.

ROTARY BLADES

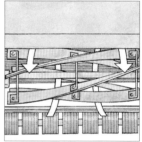

CYLINDER BLADES

MOWING PATTERNS

It is important to change your mowing pattern to avoid causing ridges, especially if using a cylinder mower with a roller or a ride-on mower. Start by mowing around the edges of the lawn where you will turn the mower at the end of each length. Alternate mowing direction at right angles or diagonally to encourage even growth.

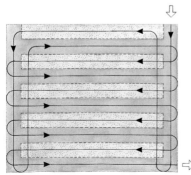

MOWING A REGULAR SHAPE

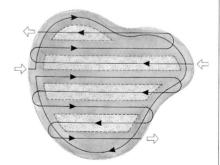

MOWING AN IRREGULAR SHAPE

WHEN TO MOW

Mowing normally begins in early spring when the cutting height should be at its maximum setting. Usually, the last cut is in late autumn, again using the maximum cutting height. In early summer, the lawn may need cutting twice a week, but once a week should do during the rest of summer.

OVERCUT LAWN
Cutting grass too closely, or "scalping", results in bald patches where grass is very susceptible to drought.

◀ BULBS IN TURF
With spring bulbs planted in grass the last cut should be late in autumn, but in spring, cutting should not begin until six weeks after flowering.

MOWING FREQUENCY

HIGH-QUALITY LAWNS		
Spring and autumn	Once or twice a week	Down to 1cm height
Summer	Up to three times a week	Down to a minimum of 8mm in early summer
UTILITY LAWNS		
Spring and autumn	Once a week	Down to about 2.5cm height
Summer	Once a week	Down to 1.5cm mimimum on lawns that are growing strongly

VALUABLE USES FOR CLIPPINGS

Grass clippings are a valuable addition to the compost heap because they are moist and rich in nitrogen. But if composted on their own they turn into an evil-smelling mass. Mix them with other coarser vegetable matter to act as an activator to decomposition. Green grass clippings make a useful mulch around vegetables and soft fruit, but if the lawn is full of seeding weeds you may spread weeds into the rest of the garden. The first two clippings from grass treated with herbicide should be disposed of (not composted or used as a mulch).

CLIPPINGS FOR COMPOST
Clippings help activate decomposition of leaves in autumn. They need to be mixed in well or can be used to cap a compost heap.

LAWN EDGES

NEVER IGNORE THE EDGE of a lawn because its neatness greatly enhances the overall appearance. Regular clipping with shears reduces the need to re-cut the edge, which you should need to do only once a year in spring. Keep surrounding plants back from the lawn or the grass will die, albeit temporarily.

NEAT AND FORMAL
The effect of this perfect green sward is enhanced by its neatly trimmed edge, which suits the formality of a small garden bed filled with scarlet pelargoniums. Such quality is not achieved without hard work and this type of lawn requires mowing at least twice a week in early summer and regular edging.

CUTTING THE EDGE OF THE LAWN

A thin strip of turf should be removed from the edge of the lawn every spring, using a half-moon edger. Cut the grass against a straight edge, such as a wooden plank, to keep the lines smooth. Alternatively, hire a machine to do the job more quickly. During the rest of the year, cut only the grass at the edge, using shears. Collect the clippings or they may root in the lawn edge "gutter" and spread into beds and paths.

EDGE-CUTTING TIPS
• Once a year re-cut the lawn edge to retain the lawn's shape and to create definition.
• Do not use a spade to cut turf edges – the curved blade will give a scalloped effect.
• At other times of the year, clip the grass at the edge of the lawn using shears.
• When clipping, angle the cut so that it is made hard against the turf edge.

TRIMMING THE EDGE
After mowing, trim the grass overhanging the edge with long-handled edging shears, or use a nylon-line trimmer adapted to work vertically.

EDGING BY HAND
If re-cutting the edge manually, use a sharp half-moon edger, cutting along the line of a plank of wood to achieve a straight edge.

EDGING BY MACHINE
For large lawns, or as a "one-off" treatment, you can hire a power edger. Align the blade along the required new edge; guide the machine forward.

How to Repair a Damaged Edge

Where small areas of a lawn edge have been damaged, they are easily repaired by cutting out sections and moving them forward so that a new, firm, clean edge can be cut. The gaps left in the lawn will need to filled. It helps if you have some spare turf, say from an unwanted patch of lawn elsewhere in the garden, but if not, use bought turf or fill the gaps with soil and sow with grass seed. The turf is firmed and the joints brushed with soil. It is then well watered until the grass is growing strongly.

1 **Undercut** the turf with a spade, then slide it forward until the damaged part is beyond the lawn edge.

2 **Align a plank** with the lawn edge, then cut along it so that the piece of turf is level with the rest of the edge.

3 **Cut a new piece** of turf to fit the resulting gap and ease it into the hole; trim it so that it forms an exact fit.

4 **Add or remove** soil beneath the new turf if necessary, until the new piece is level with the rest of the lawn.

5 **Once the level** is even, tamp the new piece into place with the back of a rake or use a medium-weight roller.

6 **Sprinkle** some sandy top-dressing over the repaired area, particularly into the joints, and water thoroughly.

ALTERNATIVE METHOD

An alternative way to patch broken edges is to cut out the turf in a neat square or rectangle, and turn it around so that the damaged area is facing away from the edge. The gap is then filled with sifted soil or sandy loam and seeds are sown on the bare area. The turf is finally firmed down and watered well to encourage new growth as the grass re-establishes.

1 **Cut a section** containing the damaged part. Turn it so that the damage faces the lawn and firm it into place.

2 **Add sandy loam** if the damaged part is not level with the rest of the lawn, sow grass seeds, and water well.

LAWN PROBLEMS

INEVITABLY PROBLEMS DEVELOP in a lawn over time, and these may be caused by the soil profile, mowing, or by general wear and tear. All these problems are usually cured by tending to the worn turf or by patching in new turf to replace it. Both remedies are best carried out in autumn, when the grass is still growing and watering is unlikely to be a problem. The grass should be sufficiently established to withstand mowing and normal wear by the following spring.

LEVELLING A HOLLOW OR HUMP

Humps on an uneven lawn surface result in patches of grass being cut too closely, causing scalping problems. Hollows leave patches of unevenly long grass. To level a small hollow or hump, cut a cross over the area, cut under the turf and peel it back. Fork the soil and remove or add some to alleviate the problem, allowing for some settling after the turf is replaced. Brush fine soil into the joints, firm, and water well.

1 **Cut a cross** right through the hump or hollow, using a half-moon edger. The edges of the cross should extend just beyond the problem area. Cut under the turf.

2 **Fold back** the undercut turf, starting at the centre of the cross and taking care not to pull the sections too harshly. Forced movements may cause the turf to crack.

3 **Fill in the ground** beneath a hollow with good, sifted, sandy topsoil. If the problem is a hump, remove some of the soil until the entire surface is level.

4 **Replace the folded-back** turf and lightly firm to check that the level is correct. Adjust the soil level beneath, if necessary, then firm, top-dress (see p.31), and water well.

How to Repair a Damaged Patch

Worn areas of lawn can be repaired by returfing or seeding. If you buy fresh turf and it looks strikingly different from the surrounding grass, lift some pieces from an inconspicuous area of the lawn for patching and replace them with the new turf. If sowing seed, fork the soil gently, sow, water and cover with clear plastic until germination.

1 **Using a half-moon edger** and the edge of a wooden plank, cut around the damaged area of lawn. Then undercut the turf with a spade and remove it completely.

2 **Lightly fork** over the exposed soil to loosen it and encourage the new turf to root into the soil. Then apply a dressing of a liquid or granular fertilizer.

3 **Carefully tread** over the soil to consolidate it and firm the surface before returfing. Place a new piece of turf in the hole, cutting it to fit with a half-moon edger.

4 **Check that** the new turf is level with the rest of the lawn. If necessary, adjust the soil level beneath the turf before pressing it into position. Then firm in the turf and water well.

Lifting Turf for Relaying

1 **Cut the turf** into strips: insert 2 short canes 30cm in from the turf edge. Stand on a plank placed flush against them and cut along it.

2 **Cut each strip** into turves about 45cm long, then undercut these to a depth of at least 2.5cm. Stack them grass-to-grass on a path or plastic.

3 **Trim the lifted** turves to the same depth: place each turf upside-down in a prepared box and slice off any soil above the correct level.

LAWN PESTS AND DISEASES

MOST LAWNS SUFFER from few pests and diseases, and these can often be tolerated on general-purpose lawns. Fine-leaved grasses can be prone to a few common diseases if they are not growing strongly – but early treatment can prevent long-term damage. Other lawn problems may be caused by the nature of the site, or by algae, moss or lichen. Always consider treating the cause of such problems, such as by improving drainage, before using chemicals.

DISEASES OF LAWNS

Fungal diseases are most prevalent if the soil is poorly drained, or if the weather is cool and wet. Good air circulation around plants discourages fungal disease, and leaves that have fallen onto the lawn should be removed as an accumulation often causes problems. Excess nitrogen applied to lawns in the autumn encourages soft growth that is susceptible to fungal disease in moist, cool weather.

HEALTH TIPS
• Use a special seasonal feed for your lawn in autumn, not a general one.
• Mow regularly.
• Clear away fallen leaves as soon as possible.
• Spray affected areas as soon a problem is noticed.

▲ AFTER DROUGHT
An arid scene like this need not necessarily be the end of the world for a lawn; rain should soon perk it up.

► EVIDENCE OF WORMS
Worms may bring casts to the lawn surface, especially in autumn. Don't kill worms; simply brush away the casts.

USING CONTROLS

Although lawn pests are not easy to control with chemicals, there are useful sprays that can be used against the most common lawn diseases. Unless the problem has been experienced in previous years, it should not be necessary to apply preventative sprays. Remember not to mow immediately before or after spraying chemicals on to the lawn, and heed manufacturers' instructions about restricting pets' access after spraying.

CHEMICALS AND SAFETY
• **Read** the instructions carefully and apply chemicals at the stated rate.
• **Store** concentrates in a safe place, away from children, and do not store diluted sprays.
• **Use** sprays on cool, windless, dry days and when the soil is moist.
• **Wear** protective clothing, especially when mixing concentrates.

COMMON PROBLEMS

▲ Cats and dogs
Urine often burns lawns; more so in dry weather. Pour water over soiled areas. Use repellents. Re-seed patches that have been badly affected.

▲ Snow mould
Fusarium patch often affects small areas, but can spread. It occurs in autumn and under compacted snow. Scarify; avoid high-nitrogen feeds in autumn.

▲ Mole hills
If you can't live with these on your lawn, mole smokes may deter, or use a trap and take your mole to some rough pasture to dig in peace.

Leatherjackets
These larvae of crane flies feed on grass roots, causing brown patches in spring and summer. Cover the lawn with a plastic sheet at night to draw them to the surface for birds to eat.

Algae
This green or black slime is a sign that the lawn is poorly drained. Lawn sand (*see p.40*) usually kills algae quickly but algae will reappear on consistently wet lawns.

Dollar spot
This fungal disease causes straw-coloured patches up to 5cm across. It is most common on fine turf and can be prevented by removing thatch through scarification.

Chafer bugs
These creamy-white, brown-headed grubs eat grass roots during the summer, but they are usually far fewer in number than leatherjackets and rarely require action.

Lichen
These flat leaf-like growths indicate impoverished soil, although shade may cause their presence. Improving the growth of the grass or applying lawn sand will help.

Toadstools
Toadstools feed on organic matter in the soil. They should be brushed off as they appear, to prevent spore production. Rings of them are difficult to control with chemicals.

▲ Red thread
Corticum is a problem only on starved, fine-leaved lawns in late summer, when leaves look bleached and covered with red threads. Strong turf, however, usually recovers.

▲ Slime mould
These strange-looking fungi are a sign that the lawn is badly drained. The surface of the lawn should be aerated or the whole site drained to prevent the mould spreading.

▲ Ant hills
These are usually a problem only on dry, sandy soils. There are chemical treatments to apply to the centres of the hills, which can be opened up using a spade.

LAWN WEEDS

M OST WEEDS WILL NOT TOLERATE regular mowing. Those that do are plants that seed and creep below the level of the mower, such as the lesser yellow trefoil. Among the most successful lawn weeds are those that form rosettes, such as plantains and dandelions, which push grass out of the way as they grow. Lawn weeds may be present in the original seedbed or be introduced with poor turf. On established lawns, seeds may blow in from borders, surface from the earth in worm casts, or be spread during mowing without a grass box.

CONTROLLING WEEDS

Regular mowing at the correct height will discourage weeds, as will regular lawn feeding and watering. Patches of coarse grass can be slashed and raked out. There are times, however, when chemical controls are necessary. Lawn sand burns broad-leaved plants, weakens small-leaved weeds and kills moss and algae. Keep grazing pets away from treated areas for a week to allow the sand to dissipate. Selective weedkillers affect broad-leaved weeds but grasses will be unaffected at the stated dose.

DESIGNED FOR WEEDING
Isolated, rosette-forming weeds can be cut out using a special "daisy-grubber". Fill the hole that is left with some sifted soil and re-seed.

IMPROMPTU TOOLS
Special tools are not essential. Cutting around with a kitchen knife will enable you to take out the entire tap root of a weed such as a dandelion.

WEEDKILLERS

Liquids These are diluted and watered onto the turf with a rose or dribble bar.
Powders and granules These are applied to turf when the soil is moist. They include weed- and moss-killers and can be spread by hand or with a wheeled spreader.
Spot weedkillers These are used to kill individual weeds in lawns and are very useful in small areas.

MOSS INFESTATIONS

Moss is common on underfed lawns and wet lawns in shade. Apply a moss-killer in spring and rake out the dead moss. Moss-killers can be used in autumn, but scarifying at this time can spread the problem. If the soil is poor and acid, try applying lime. Feed the lawn to encourage grass growth.

► PERSISTENT MOSS
If moss is a recurrent problem, the soil may need draining; in dense shade, grass may be replaced by ground cover or even a moss lawn.

KNOW YOUR WEED

Field bindweed
This weed spreads by creeping, underground shoots and can be quite a problem in poor soils. Use a weedkiller to control it.

Common white clover
Regular feeding and watering in dry weather will help to prevent clover from spreading. Applications of weedkiller will also control it.

Slender speedwell
A weed that prefers moist soil and can be difficult to control with selective weedkillers, although lawn sand usually weakens it.

Dandelion
The rosettes of leaves smother grasses, and plants quickly self-seed. If the problem is localized, spot-treat or hand-weed (*see left*).

Creeping buttercup
This weed is common on moist, clay soils. Small areas can be hand-weeded, but using selective weedkillers is also effective.

Sheep's sorrel
This weed indicates poor, dry, acid soil. Regular feeding and watering will reduce it. Weedkillers must be used repeatedly for control.

Broad-leaved plantain
This weed forms broad, grass-smothering rosettes. Individual plants can easily be cut out of the turf, as with dandelions, or spot-treated.

Yarrow
Yarrow is often evident on poor, dry soils. Repeated weedkiller applications weaken it, and small areas may be forked out.

Lesser yellow trefoil
This annual weed is quickly spread by mowing without a grass box. Repeated use of weedkiller should control this problem.

LAWN RENOVATION

WITH CONTINUED NEGLECT, A LAWN may get to the stage where a decision has to be made about its future. Irregular and close mowing, drought, dogs, excessive wear, and the build-up of thatch, moss and weeds all take their toll on a lawn. A worn-out lawn not only looks unsightly, but it also spoils the look of the whole garden. If all areas of the lawn are in a bad state it is probably best to remove and replace the lawn rather than trying to renovate it.

IS YOUR LAWN WORTH SAVING?

Patching the lawn may rejuvenate areas but, even if patches are properly prepared, they will stand out as good turf amid the surrounding rough grass. Top-dressing, weed-killing, feeding and irrigation may renovate lawns that are not too badly neglected. Find out why your lawn is in poor condition before deciding to replace the grass. Persistent drought or shade may mean that a lawn will never grow, as may recurrent problems such as severe moss infestation or multiple fairy rings (*below*).

▲ EXTREME CONDITIONS
If your lawn fails completely due to drought or shade, it may be more sensible to take up the turf and lay a hard surface or gravel, perhaps with some tough ground cover plants.

RESCUING A LAWN

- **Discover** the reason for the poor quality of the turf.
- **Cut** the lawn at your mower's highest setting, reducing the height each week.
- **Give** the turf a lawn tonic to stimulate growth (*see p.28*).
- **Aerate** the turf to reduce soil compaction (*see p.31*).
- **Brush** in top-dressing (*see p.31*).
- **Apply** weedkiller if necessary.
- **Scarify** the lawn in autumn (*see p.30*).
- **Kill** moss in autumn (*see p.40*).
- **Patch** worn areas with new turf in autumn or spring (*see p.37*).
- **Drain** waterlogged soil (*see p.16*).

If a lawn should need to be replaced, spray the whole area with a total weedkiller. Dig over the ground, and take measures to alleviate any soil problems. Prepare the soil by treading and raking, and sow seed or lay new turf in autumn.

FAIRY RINGS
These are caused by fungi that feed on organic matter in the soil. They form a dense layer of fungal growth that is impervious to water and very difficult to kill with chemicals.

PERSISTENT MOSS
On waterlogged, acid or poor soil, and in shade, moss will flourish instead of grass. Moss-killers are effective but, without changing soil conditions, moss will regrow.

LAWNS IN THE SHADE OF TREES

Lawns often suffer under trees because of the shade they cast and the drought caused by their roots. A more attractive alternative is often to clear a circle of ground beneath and plant it with shade-tolerant ground cover plants. But if you really want to have grass growing right up to the tree, cut away the damaged area and re-sow or re-turf it. Use shade-tolerant turf, if possible, or a seed mixture suitable for shade. After sowing seed, cover the area with netting.

REPLANTING UNDER TREES
To plant ground cover or renew the grass, cut away a suitable area. Remove sufficient soil and any weeds and fork in a general fertilizer.

SEASONAL CARE CHART

SPRING

Rake the grass to remove debris, but do not scarify to remove thatch.

Mow the lawn, cutting to the maximum height at first, and gradually lowering the height as the season progresses.

Roll lawns to level high areas raised by frost heave.

Repair and re-shape lawn edges.

Apply moss-killers, such as lawn sand and weedkillers.

Apply lawn feeds in moist weather.

Irrigate the lawn in dry weather.

Prepare sites for new lawns. Lay turf or sow from seed.

SUMMER

Mow the lawn regularly, at the correct height, but raise the height of the cut in dry weather.

Keep edges trimmed.

Irrigate if possible in dry weather, giving a thorough soak each week. Irrigating new lawns is particularly important.

Apply a weedkiller, if necessary, when the soil is moist.

Aerate areas that are severely compacted.

Feed the lawn in moist weather and apply a lawn tonic after wet weather.

Cut out lawn weeds and apply weedkillers in moist weather.

AUTUMN

Apply a seasonal feed.

Reduce the frequency of mowing and raise the height of the cut.

Brush away worm casts before mowing.

Scarify lawns to remove thatch and moss.

Aerate compacted areas of lawns.

Prepare sites for new lawns and sow seed.

Lay turf for a new lawn.

Make any necessary lawn repairs.

Apply top-dressings.

Sweep up and remove fallen leaves.

Treat fungal lawn diseases.

Plant bulbs for naturalizing in grass.

WINTER

Service mowers and other lawn equipment.

Sweep up and remove fallen leaves from the lawn.

Lay turf in mild weather.

Keep off the lawn in frosty weather.

NON-GRASS LAWNS

GRASS MAY BE THE MOST ADAPTABLE and cheapest plant with which to create a lawn, but it is not the only option. Other plants with a spreading habit can withstand the occasional footfall, if not frequent treading. Most are more selective than grass about growing conditions or soil. They are best restricted to small areas because they do not always form dense, complete cover, so hand weeding may be necessary (selective lawn weedkillers cannot be used).

BOUQUET OF SCENTS
This small lawn is not a major route across the garden and receives little wear. The mixture of camomile and thyme forms a weed-smothering mat that is attractive all year, and is colourful with bloom in summer. Treading releases sweet and spicy scents that mingle with the perfume of the surrounding flowers.

WHICH PLANTS TO USE?

The non-flowering camomile 'Treneague' is the ideal choice for an alternative lawn, but creeping Corsican mint (*Mentha requienii*) and low-growing thymes such as *Thymus doerfleri* and *T. serpyllum* are also fragrant and effective. Beware of thyme lawns in family gardens, however; the flowers will attract a great many bees to the garden. If the lawn is to be purely decorative and rarely walked on, other small, spreading plants (*right*) can be used to create the effect of a "living carpet". Moss (*see p.40*) is also an option on damp, shady ground.

ALTERNATIVES TO HERBS
• **Cotula** Creeping plants with finely divided leaves and small, "button" flowers.
• **Mind-your-own-business** *Soleirolia soleirolii* spreads rampantly on moist soils in mild areas.
• **Dichondra** A creeping plant with tiny flowers, for frost-free gardens only.
• **Pearlwort** *Sagina*, a weed in some gardens; there is a pretty golden-leaved form.
• **Acaena** Hard-wearing, tolerating some treading, but with prickly seedheads.
• **Ophiopogon** Use black-leaved, grass-like *O. planiscapus* 'Nigrescens' for dramatic effect.

NON-FLOWERING CAMOMILE

LOW-GROWING THYMES

CREEPING MINT

What Maintenance is Necessary?

Although a non-grass lawn will not need mowing, it does require some care, and it can be an expensive option unless you raise your own plants (*see overleaf*). Make sure your plant choice suits your soil (*see* Good Plants for Ground Cover, *pp.64–77*), and first clear the ground of both perennial and annual weeds (*see p.58*). Space the plants 20–30cm apart, planting with as much care as you would in a bed or border (*see p.59*). Water regularly until established, and weed around the young plants. Most plants will benefit from an application of general fertilizer in spring, and a trim in early spring or in late summer. Long-handled or one-handed shears (*below*) may make the job easier.

SINGLE-HANDED SHEARS

LONG-HANDLED SHEARS

FRAGRANT CORNER
Keep the area of alternative lawns small so that maintenance by hand does not become a chore. After several years the lawn will need to be remade and the soil enriched.

Adding Taller Plants

You can use creeping herbs to create ribbons of low ground cover between other plants. Taller herbs such as santolina will accentuate the theme of the planting, and clumps of ornamental grasses add vertical interest. You could also use low plants to form "rivers" of greenery in rock gardens, or among paving or gravel, as many enjoy a sunny site with free-draining soil. Small bulbs can be added to create seasonal interest. Crocuses in particular can create striking contrasts: try orange ones in camomile, blue in *Soleirolia* 'Aurea' or white in black-leaved *Ophiopogon*.

LEVELS OF INTEREST
If it is not walked on often, the alternative lawn does not have to be completely flat, and you can use dwarf shrubs.

GROWING PLANTS FOR HERB LAWNS

Raising your own plants for herb lawns makes good economic sense, provided that you have room to care for seedlings and plantlets. Having young plants to hand also means you can replace casualties and old plants past their best. You can divide large plants to make smaller plants that will soon grow together, or you can grow others from seed and cuttings. Plants from seed are not always identical to the parent.

PLANTS TO RAISE YOURSELF

• Camomile can be grown from seed, and clumps of the dwarf 'Treneague' are easily split into rooted sections (*see p.61*).
• Thymes can be grown from seed, or from cuttings taken in summer.
• Golden marjoram (*Origanum vulgare* 'Aureum') can be increased by cuttings taken in summer or by dividing plants in spring.

SOWING SEED IN POTS

1 Fill a 13cm pot with moist seed compost. Firm the compost to about 1cm below the rim. Using a folded piece of paper, scatter the seeds sparingly over the compost. Cover the seeds with a layer of sieved compost or grit, label, and water gently.

2 Cover the pot with a sheet of glass or clear plastic, or enclose it in a plastic bag, and leave it on a greenhouse bench or a cool windowsill. As the seedlings sprout, thin them until you have only 5 or 6 good strong ones per pot, evenly spaced. Alternatively, you can transplant some of the thinned seedlings into trays, to grow on more plants.

SOWING SEED IN TRAYS

If you have the room (greenhouse shelving or staging, for example) you can grow "turves" of camomile to plant out in one piece by sowing in trays, and thinning the resulting seedlings to about 4cm apart. Once the plants are growing well, put the trays outside in the daytime and bring them in at night for a few days before you plant to acclimatize them to outdoor conditions. Plant the turves in shallow trenches about 10cm apart. Fork over the soil in the base of the trench with a handfork and water it well before planting and firming in, so that the roots of the young plants can easily establish.

Wait until seedlings have two true leaves before thinning

Scatter the seeds evenly

Dividing Clump-forming Plants

A large plant, such as a big mound of thyme, can be lifted in spring or autumn and divided into several smaller pieces that, by the end of the following summer, will cover at least four times more ground than did the original clump (*see also* Division,

p.61). Careful division, and replanting into fresh soil, rejuvenates the plant and stimulates new growth. You can do this with large, container-grown specimens bought at garden centres, and these are often better value than small plants.

1 Dig up the plant, shake off the loose soil, then trim back the top-growth so that the clump is easier to handle and the soft tips are removed.

2 Cut or pull the clump into sections, discarding any old woody parts from the centre that are leafless and have no young roots.

3 Replant the divisions in fresh soil or a site that has been enriched with organic matter and fertilizer. Water immediately after planting.

Growing on Plantlets

Even if you are not experienced in taking cuttings, growing small, rooted pieces of larger plants separated from their parent in spring or early summer is very easy. Mints have creeping roots that sprout at many points (*see right*). Mounding old, woody thymes (*see below*) is another method of layering (*see p.63*) that can produce dozens of young plants. Work a gritty compost mix between the shoots, and water thoroughly to encourage rooting.

New shoot

Long mint roots have many growing points

MINT RUNNERS
Dig up a creeping mint root, shake off the soil, and you should be able to section it into several plantlets, each with one or two growing shoots.

MOUNDING THYME
In spring, trickle a mixture of peat and coarse sand into the crown of the plant, shaking the stems. Water in dry spells.

SEVERING ROOTED STEMS
After a few months, gently uncover the stems to find that roots have sprouted. Sever the rooted shoots and grow on.

GROWING ON

Fill a seed tray with a compost mix suitable for cuttings, firm it and insert the plantlets. Water them well, and keep the tray on a cool, light windowsill (in winter), or in a cold frame in spring or summer. Water gently but well whenever the compost surface seems dry. New plants should be large enough to plant out the following spring, or a few months after potting.

WILDFLOWER MEADOWS

A MEADOW IS A LAWN that is managed so that plants other than grass are encouraged. The style suits rural gardens perfectly, but even a small area in a town garden, carefully managed so that it looks attractive and colourful, and not like a piece of waste ground, provides a breath of the countryside and a valuable refuge for wildlife in an urban setting. Long grass provides food for many caterpillars and a home for insects that help to control garden pests.

DIFFERENT STYLES OF MEADOW PLANTING

Your ideal meadow may well be populated by what some people would consider weeds, but they must be the right kind of weeds, and this needs careful planning and some management. You may also wish to add more conventional border plants and bulbs and to encourage them to naturalize informally. The effects you create can also be planned to vary with the seasons.

◀ TINY TREASURES
Fritillaries will thrive and spread in moist grassland, and flower in spring when the grass is short.

▲ TALL GRASS
By summer, large flowering plants will bloom among and above grasses and their flower spikelets.

CREATING THE RIGHT CONDITIONS

The important point to remember about wildflowers is that they need poor soil, so you need to think in a completely different way to when gardening conventionally. You must not improve or add nutrients to the soil as you would in beds and borders, nor feed, scarify, aerate or top-dress as you would a lawn. The kind of regime needed to maintain a meadow is not labour-intensive, but it may encourage undesirable weeds among the wildflowers and these will need to be removed.

REDUCING SOIL FERTILITY

When converting an area of the garden to meadow, for the best results it is worth first reducing the soil's fertility. Skim off the top 15cm or so of topsoil, including any existing turf (you may be able to use these elsewhere in the garden). This has the added advantage of removing any weeds and their seeds. To reduce nitrogen levels further, dig in uncomposted wood chips or bark. Wildflower meadows really do flourish on the poorest of soils, even on subsoil.

Choosing Plants for Your Soil

Because a meadow is a more natural environment than a lawn, and it is to be hoped that the plants you introduce will naturalize, account must be taken of your soil conditions and what will thrive in them. It is well worth taking a look at local wild areas, perhaps with the aid of a good wildflower guide, to see what grows well locally. A moist area will support different plants to dry chalkland, and working with your soil will make it easier to establish plants. But however authentic you wish your meadow to be, never be tempted to dig up plants from the wild.

ESTABLISHED MEADOWS
Specialized plants such as these terrestrial orchids will only flourish where conditions suit them, and are usually an indicator that the meadow is ancient and has been well cared for. An old meadow will have a richly diverse flora and be home to a wide range of insects. However, even a young meadow can be a useful oasis for wildlife and, with time, more plants will encroach from the surrounding countryside.

What Maintenance is Necessary?

Having a meadow is not an excuse for not mowing. It must be cut twice a year, in early summer, after spring flowers have set seed, and again in late autumn. Mowings must be raked up and removed (the equivalent of being grazed off by animals), to prevent their nutrients being added to the soil and encouraging coarse grasses at the expense of wildflowers. Most lawnmowers will not be able to cope with such long grass. The traditional mowing tool is a scythe, but this is a dangerous tool and a nylon-line trimmer is much safer for small areas – or, hire a long-grass mower.

▶ TRIMMING TOOL
A nylon-line trimmer is a practical tool to trim small areas of long grass before they are cut again with a normal mower.

▶ ONTO THE HEAP
Unlike grass clippings, meadow mowings can be put straight on the compost heap, or dry them for hay for pets.

CONVERTING EXISTING GRASS

Part of an existing lawn can be converted into a meadow, and it need not be a sunny area. It is difficult to sow flower seeds into the turf and the best results are usually achieved by planting young plants into the grass in spring or autumn, after the grass has been cut. Some will flourish and self-seed though others, that are not so well suited to your conditions, may disappear and will have to be replanted if you want to grow them. The cutting of the grass and removing the hay will prevent the soil from becoming too rich, and the flowers will begin to dominate the grasses in time to create a balanced population of plants.

WEED OR FLOWER?
Some wildflowers can be too much of a good thing, though as grass grows long and other plants are introduced, dandelions will not be able to compete as well as they can on lawns.

SUN OR SHADE
Choose wildflowers with care for sun (ox-eye daisies, above) or shade (foxgloves, left) so that they thrive and soon spread and multiply.

ADDING BULBS

Although not strictly native, many bulbs look right in a meadow, and a wide range will flourish and may self-seed. Bulbs add greatly to the period of colour, and if the grass is cut in early autumn, autumn-flowering crocuses and colchicums can be included. Small-flowered bulbs generally look more natural than large hybrids.

SELECTING SOURCES
Buy bluebells (right) and snowdrops from reputable sources: unscrupulous collecting from the wild is a serious conservation issue.

PLANTING PLUG PLANTS

You can grow your own small plants for your meadow from seed, but young plug plants are readily available and are a convenient way to plant a meadow area. Most wildflowers are sold by their common names so it is easy to get what you need. Plant in small groups in the turf rather than dotting them at regular intervals. Cut the grass immediately before planting to give them maximum light. Water well after planting.

PRIMROSES (*PRIMULA VULGARIS*)

1 **Make individual holes** for the tiny plants; a coring tool (*above*) saves work when planting in large numbers.

2 **Each of the plug plants** will have its own self-contained root system and must be kept moist.

3 **Plant and firm in** gently with your fingers, then water well for the next few weeks until growing strongly.

ADDING INTERESTING GRASSES

To give your meadow an unusual look, you can add ornamental grasses. There are many to choose from, and the ornamental forms of wild grasses can look attractive if left uncut. If you are looking for a natural effect, avoid variegated plants, which look too "tamed" and dominate the meadow.

SUITABLE GRASSES

Miscanthus There are many attractive *Miscanthus sinensis*, such as 'Grosse Fontäne' and 'Silberfeder', that create large, arching tufts of leaves and flowers.

Deschampsia The many variations of *D. cespitosa* create colourful tufts of foliage with narrow, elegant plumes of flowers.

Festucas, such as *F. glauca* (right), prefer dry soil; their blue colour needs careful siting.

STARTING FROM SCRATCH WITH SEED MIXTURES

A meadow can be made from scratch with pre-selected mixtures of grasses and wildflowers offered for sale as meadow mixes, or by sowing a mixture of wildflower seeds first, then adding grass seed once the flowering plants are established. You could also grow some perennial wildflowers in pots (*see p.63*) to add as young plants, giving them a better start. The effect may be a bit patchy in the first year, but as plants become established they will spread and fill the ground.

MEADOW MIXES
An average seed mixture contains easy-going, tough wildflowers such as poppies, cornflowers and corn cockles. These wildflowers are mostly annuals that perpetuate themselves by self-seeding each year until the growth is too dense for them to penetrate. They may also seed themselves into beds and borders. Don't worry about them seeding into conventional lawn areas, because they will not tolerate the regular mowing.

PREPARING THE GROUND

You must clear sites infested with perennial weeds such as ground elder (*see also p.58*). It is now simple to clear weeds from soil with chemicals that allow seeding and planting as soon as the dead weeds have been cleared. If you do not wish to use chemicals, hand digging and clearing (*see p.58*) is effective, but laborious. If the weed growth is not too high it can be covered with black plastic sheeting, which deprives the weeds of light and kills them after several weeks. Hoe off annual weeds.

◄ GRASP THE NETTLE
Perennial weeds such as stinging nettles must be removed at the start or they will become a problem later.

▲ CONTROL WEEDS
A slow but simple way to kill weeds is to cover the soil with a smothering layer of black plastic sheeting.

SOWING THE SEED

Do not dig over the ground deeply and add organic matter as if you were going to sow a regular lawn or you will make the soil too rich. But it greatly helps good seed germination if you break up the surface soil and rake it to a fine tilth. Once you have done so, water it and allow the annual weed seeds on the surface to germinate. Hoe these off or spray with weedkiller, rake again and then sow the seed mix. Protect this from birds as you would ordinary grass with netting, fleece or scarers (*see p.19*).

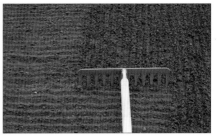

1 **Scatter the seed** over the earth, having watered first if the soil is dry. Sow thinly, in several directions to ensure an even spread of the different types of seed within the mix.

2 **Rake over** the soil in several directions to cover the seed, and water in, using a fine spray or sprinkler so that the seed is not washed from the soil. Protect against birds.

COLLECTING SEED

Once your seeds come up and flower you can tinker with the mix by collecting seed of dominant plants and disposing of it, or by cutting early, before it is shed, or sowing it elsewhere to redistribute flowers. Collect seed of plants that are struggling and grow young plants in pots to put in the next year.

◀ COLLECT SEED
If you want to choose where new plants will grow, cut off the seedheads as soon as they are ripe and collect the seed in paper bags tied over the heads.

▲ POPPY TIME
In the early stages of the meadow, poppies may be common. As the competition for space grows, they will disappear, but seeds will be in the soil, waiting to grow.

PLANTING GROUND COVER

PLANNING AND PLANT CHOICE

EVERY GARDEN HAS AREAS where grass and many garden plants have difficulty in growing, and these are where tough ground cover plants – creeping or clumping herbaceous plants, shrubs and climbers – are most useful. Ground cover may not be a miracle cure for weeds, but the more or less complete soil cover these plants provide will do a good job of suppressing them.

WHICH PLANTS TO USE?

Municipal landscapers use ground cover to beautify areas that would otherwise be covered with hard surfaces, but frequently use large expanses of one type of plant, often tough shrubs that are dull for much of the year. Ground cover in gardens need not be so unimaginative and should please the eye – much more than just a substitute for grass. There is no need to use just one plant. You can create colourful effects by mixing shrubs, perennials and bulbs.

WHY GROUND COVER?

• Ground cover plants suppress weeds and look attractive throughout the year.
• Ground cover prevents the leaching of nutrients caused by rainfall on bare earth.
• The consolidating effect of roots helps prevent soil erosion on slopes and banks.
• Ground cover can form a useful habitat for small mammals and insects.
• Plants are easier and often cheaper to "install" than hard landscaping materials.

SEA OF BLUE
This dense sward of prostrate junipers is colourful throughout the year and forms impenetrable cover. Annual weeds have no chance of seeding through the network of branches and all year, the only maintenance required is the occasional cutting back of shoots at the edge of the planting.

◀ PLANTING UNDER TREES *In shade, ground cover can mimic the natural flora of a woodland floor.*

CONSIDERING YOUR OPTIONS

Choosing ground cover that will be really successful in your site needs thought. If you are investing in quantities of plants, not to mention the work of planting them, it is not worth risking the disappointment of choosing plants that do not thrive. Well-chosen shrubs may be slow to mature, but they then provide long-lasting, labour-saving cover. Perennials usually grow and mingle faster, but after a few years, will need dividing and sometimes replacing. They are a good semi-permanent option for areas that you have more ambitious future plans for. If you need temporary cover, for a year or even a season, while you decide what to do with a site or perhaps while you propagate shrubs and perennials to occupy it, consider a temporary planting, or simply peg down thick black plastic to cover the soil – anything rather than leaving it bare.

FACTORS TO CONSIDER

• How permanent do you want the planting to be, and how long can you wait? Some of the best ground cover plants spread slowly and must be planted as young plants, close together. Fast-spreaders may be almost as invasive as the weeds they are replacing, and often need dividing and replanting to stay healthy. They may overstep their bounds and become a real nuisance in small areas.
• How little maintenance do you want to do? Mixed plantings tend to need more work than single-plant cover, to keep a balance, and interplanting with bulbs takes time too.
• Is the site in view all year? If so, opt for evergreen shrubs or perennials, and make an effort to use plants that have more than one season of interest, or combine plants with different seasons of interest.
• What other plants are nearby? You can choose ground cover to complement them, or provide interest when they are dull.

PLANTS FOR TEMPORARY COVER

If you need to cover the ground quickly while propagating plants for permanent planting, annual plants can be used. Low-growing annuals such as limnanthes, iberis and alyssum can be used to cover the soil and although they will self-seed, they will eventually be smothered by the permanent planting. Green manures are fast-growing plants that are often sown in autumn, on land cleared of perennial weeds. In winter they prevent leaching of nutrients and before they flower, they are dug into the soil to increase its fertility.

▲ GREEN MANURING
Sow seed of green manures on fallow ground. Cut the plants to the ground when 20cm tall, digging them in, when wilted, after a day.

TREFOIL

ITALIAN RYE GRASS

◀ GREEN MANURE CROPS
These plants can be useful to improve soil texture and nutrient content. Legumes such as trefoil and clover add nitrogen to poor, dry soils when dug in. Italian rye grass, mustard and phacelia add bulk to poor, heavy soils.

MATCHING PLANTS TO PLACES

For ground cover plants to do their job and look good, they must be as well-suited to their site as the weeds they are replacing. Assess the texture and structure of the soil, and how dry it is in summer. You can buy kits from garden centres that will tell you its pH (acidity or alkalinity). Look at sun and shade: for example, do not plant grey-leaved plants that need bright sunlight in shade because they will not thrive. You can mix as many plants as you like, provided that all enjoy the same conditions.

◄ DRY BANK
On a dry, exposed bank, where the soil is acidic, heathers make evergreen cover, needing just an annual clip after flowering.

▲ COOL SHADE
These hostas will unfurl to create a weed-smothering blanket. Hostas prefer moist soil; those with blue leaves are more drought-tolerant.

PLANTS FOR DIFFICULT SITES *(see also pp.64–77)*

DRY SHADE	DAMP SHADE	HOT, DRY SITES	POOR SOIL
Bergenia Large, glossy leaves and pink flowers	**Arctostaphylos** Low, berrying shrub with small leaves	**Artemisia** Grey-leaved perennials and shrubs	**Anthemis** Feathery leaves and daisy-like flowers
Euonymus Bright, often variegated, evergreen shrubs	**Hellebore** Deep green leaves, and flowers in winter	**Cerastium** Invasive, with silver leaves and white flowers	**Cistus** Aromatic foliage and pretty, papery flowers
Ivy (*Hedera*) Green and variegated creepers for low cover	**Mahonia** Evergreen with yellow flower spires in winter	**Genista** Green stems and yellow flowers	**Galium** Tiny, with delicate foliage and small, white flowers
Lamium Bright foliage and cottagey flower spikes	**Sarcococca** Fragrant, dense, evergreen shrubs	**Nepeta** Aromatic, with grey leaves and sprays of blue flowers	**Hypericum** Shrubby, low and spreading, with yellow flowers
Pachysandra Neat, evergreen cover	**Saxifrage** Rosettes of leaves and delicate white flowers	**Osteospermum** Daisy-like flowers and evergreen leaves	**Lavender** Scented, grey leaves and blue flowers
Vinca Fast grower, with blue flowers	**Tolmiea** Dense, bristly foliage	**Stachys** Furry, grey "lamb's-ear" leaves	**Sedum** Fleshy foliage and starry flowers

Preparation and Planting

ALTHOUGH MANY GROUND COVER plants will tolerate poor soil, most will not thrive. Ground cover plants should be in their position for many years. If they are to grow vigorously and prevent an influx of weeds, the soil must be prepared thoroughly, and in addition to removing all perennial weeds, the soil should be enriched with organic matter and general fertilizer. Choose plants that are suited to the soil type and situation so they spread as fast as possible.

Clearing Ground Weeds

Annual weeds can be cleared from the site by hoeing, or by using a contact weedkiller. Perennial weeds, however, require more care. Even small pieces of root may grow and spread through the newly-planted ground cover. Carefully fork out the roots of perennials such as bindweed and ground elder, spray with a translocated weedkiller, or suppress growth with black plastic.

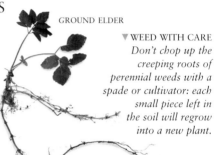

GROUND ELDER

▼ WEED WITH CARE
Don't chop up the creeping roots of perennial weeds with a spade or cultivator: each small piece left in the soil will regrow into a new plant.

USING WEEDKILLERS

• Use the product as recommended by the manufacturer and at the correct season for best results.
• Never use at a greater concentration than instructed.
• Apply weedkillers on overcast, dry days when there is little wind, especially when using a sprayer.
• Wear protective clothing: gloves, goggles and rubber boots.

Digging Over and Improving Soil

Once perennial weeds have been cleared from the planting area, it can be dug over to improve the structure and to dig in organic matter. A rotary cultivator will quickly incorporate organic matter over a large area. First spread the compost on the surface and run over with the cultivator. This will give a fine tilth that is easy to plant into. Fork the compost into smaller areas by hand, breaking up large clods.

▶ IMPROVING STRUCTURE
To improve soil structure, dig in organic material, such as well-rotted manure or compost, according to the needs of the soil.

PLANTING

Water plants thoroughly before planting, then space them on the soil. Dig out the planting hole and fill it with water to soak the soil. Knock the plant from the pot and, if the plant is dormant, tease out the roots before putting it in the hole. Keep the soil level as it was in the pot. After planting, give the plants another soak with water and then mulch around them (*below*). On banks, leave a ring of raised soil around the plants to make it easier to irrigate without water running down the slope.

1 Dig a hole twice the width of the plant's root ball. Mix the removed soil with organic matter. Check the soil level using a cane, and adjust.

2 Carefully support the plant as you ease it out of its container and into the hole. Backfill around the shrub with the soil mixture.

3 Once the hole has been filled, carefully firm the soil around the plant using either your heel or your hands. Water well.

MULCHING BETWEEN PLANTS

Mulches reduce moisture loss from the soil and help to suppress weeds. Bark mulch lasts a long time but is low in nutrients. Garden compost and spent mushroom compost are good soil conditioners, but do not last as long. Mulch immediately after planting, and every year after pruning or in spring.

▶ MULCH GENEROUSLY
A thin layer of mulch will not really do the job. Ideally, it should be about 10–15cm deep.

SHEET MULCHING

Planting through black plastic or planting membrane controls weeds over a large area and maintains soil moisture. A layer of bark or gravel will disguise it.

PLANTS AND PLASTIC
• Remember that plants that spread by creeping roots and runnering stems will not be able to do so through plastic.
• Planting single bulbs through plastic is impossible. Instead, cut out a circle and plant the bulbs in a group.

1 Insert a plant through a slit in the plastic using a trowel. Firm the soil by the roots and water.

2 Apply a decorative mulch on top of the plastic sheeting to a depth of at least 5cm.

ROUTINE CARE

LIKE ANY OTHER young plants, new ground cover needs some attention to keep it looking neat and healthy: hand weeding to remove any perennial or annual weeds; regular feeding to encourage strong growth; watering while the new plants are getting established, especially under trees or in dry sites. Once established, it will need an annual trim or tidy and a mulch, and division of perennials and bulbs.

TRIMMING AND PRUNING

It is often not practical to prune individual stems, except perhaps wayward branches of shrubs. Many plants can be sheared in spring or after flowering; herbaceous plants, and some creeping shrubs like vinca and *Hypericum calycinum* can be cut with a line trimmer. Rake off the prunings. Always let fading bulb leaves die down naturally.

AFTERCARE

• After raking away prunings and any dead branches, cover ("top-dress") the soil between herbaceous plants with compost and apply general fertilizer to encourage growth.
• If the weather is dry after pruning, irrigate the bed to ensure strong growth.

PRUNING GREY-LEAVED SHRUBS
Cut back old shoots immediately after flowering or in spring to expose new leafy growth at the base of the plant.

ROTARY LINE TRIMMER
The flexible nylon cutting line rotates at high speed to cut through soft-stemmed plants; goggles and stout trousers are recommended.

PRUNING GROUND-COVER ROSES

Ground-cover roses (*see also p.69*) do not need the strict pruning usually recommended for bush roses. The shrubby, bushy types need virtually none, except to cut off any unhealthy or dead stems whenever you see them. The vigorous rambler types can get out of hand; you may need to trim them to keep them within bounds, and their long, whippy new arching shoots can be a nuisance (*right*). You can pin these down (*inset*), which encourages them to flower better and sometimes to root and spread; if the clump is getting crowded, remove a few older flowered stems completely.

RAMBLER-TYPE GROUND-COVER ROSE
Wearing gloves, draw long stems carefully down to ground level and secure them on the soil with a length of wire bent into a hoop

DIVIDING CLUMPS OF PERENNIALS

Most perennials are easy to propagate by division. This should be done in autumn or spring while the plants are dormant or just coming into growth. The outer parts of the clumps are the most vigorous, and the inner, older part is usually discarded.

DIVIDE IN SPRING

Plants that prefer well-drained soil and are slightly tender are best divided in spring.
• *Agapanthus* • *Ajuga* • *Anthemis*
• *Artemisia* • *Asarum*• *Chamaemelum*
• *Hosta* • *Lamium* • *Liriope*
• *Houttuynia* • *Nepeta* • *Sedum*
• *Stachys* • *Tanacetum*

DIVIDE IN AUTUMN

Most plants can be divided in autumn, when the soil is still warm and moist. Spring-flowering plants will have longer to get established before they bloom.
• *Bergenia* • *Brunnera* • *Campanula*
• *Convallaria* • *Dicentra* • *Epimedium*
• *Geranium* • *Helleborus* • *Hemerocallis*
• *Heuchera* • *Pulmonaria* • *Symphytum*
• *Tiarella* • *Trachystemon*

HAND DIVISION
After lifting, many plants can simply be split by pulling the clump apart by hand.

USING A SPADE
Thick root clumps can be cut first with a knife or spade to part the new shoots.

DIVIDING PLANTS WITH FLESHY ROOTS

Agapanthus, acanthus, iris and bergenias have thick roots that may rot if damaged in autumn and replanted into cold, wet soil. To prevent this, either wait until spring to move the plants or divide them in autumn and pot on the divisions, keeping them in a cold frame until spring.

BERGENIAS
These creeping perennials send up plantlets on thick, woody stems that can be cut or snapped off the parent and replanted, horizontally, in a new place.

DIVIDING BULBS

Bulbs that are planted under ground cover, to give extra colour, are difficult to find when they have died down. Fortunately, they will come to no harm if lifted and split while they are in leaf, after the flowers have faded. Divide into small groups or individual bulbs. Replant as soon as possible so that the roots do not dry out.

▶ DIVIDING BY HAND
Divide a clump of bulbs by hand, separating it first into smaller clumps and then into individual bulbs. Remove any dead material.

MAKING MORE OF YOUR PLANTS

PLANTING LARGE AREAS of ground cover requires dozens, even hundreds, of plants. This can make a project expensive, but if you plan ahead you can propagate your own plants. Division (*see previous page*) or layering produces identical plants for an even effect, but raising plants from seed is also easy.

SEVERING ROOTED PLANTLETS

Some plants have stems that root where they touch the ground and you can exploit this by encouraging the rooting and then severing the new plants to put into new areas. If the severed part is very small and you have a greenhouse or cold frame, you can pot it up and grow it on for a season, to give it a better start when planted out.

ROOTING STEMS

- *Hedera* (ivies)
- *Hypericum calycinum*
- *Lysimachia nummularia*
- *Mahonia*
- *Pachysandra*
- Roses, rambler types
- *Rubus tricolor*
- *Vinca major*
- *Vinca minor*

1 **Select** a low-growing shoot that has rooted into the ground and lift the rooted section with a hand fork.

2 **Sever the shoot** from the parent plant (here an ivy, *Hedera*), cutting between the leaf joints with secateurs.

3 **Cut the shoot** into sections, each with a healthy root system and vigorous new growth. Remove the lower leaves.

4 **Replant each** section of rooted shoot either into a pot of cutting compost or in its permanent position.

SUCKERING SHRUBS

1 **Select a shoot** that is growing from below ground, lift the rooted section, and sever from the parent.

2 **Cut the** shoot into sections, each with a healthy root system and vigorous growth.

3 **Replant each section** of rooted shoot either into a pot of cutting compost or in its permanent position.

LAYERING STEMS

Pinning down a stem from a self-rooting or suckering plant, such as clematis, cotoneaster, lavender, thyme, trachelospermum or *Vitis coignetiae*, often encourages it to develop roots. Cut a tongue in the stem (*see below*) where it will touch the soil. Make a hollow. and mix some coarse grit into the soil. Peg the stem in place. Cover with compost and water well. Rooting may take up to a year.

Wire peg holds shoot in place

LAYERED STEM
Brought into contact with the soil, the shoot develops its own roots, fed by the parent plant.

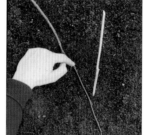

1 **Bring a young** stem down to the soil and mark its position. Dig a hole by the mark about 8cm deep, with a slight slope toward the parent.

2 **Trim off** shoots and leaves on the stem and cut a tongue of bark on its underside to contact the soil. Apply rooting hormone to the cut.

3 **Peg down** the stem to the soil. Bend up the stem's tip vertically and secure it to the cane with a tie. Fill the hole with soil, firm, and water.

SOWING SEED

You do not need high temperatures to grow many seeds, and a simple cold frame is ideal. Because some hardy plants take a long time to germinate, use a soil-based compost, cover with grit (which discourages moss growth) and plunge the pots into damp sand, to maintain steady moisture. Some hardy plants require a cool period in winter, so sow in autumn and leave the pots outside until the seedlings appear in spring. Not all plants grow true to type from seed, but the variations can be beautiful, especially with hellebores.

COLLECT YOUR OWN SEED

You can gather seed from the following.
• Achillea • Agapanthus • Alchemilla
• Cotula • Dicentra • Hardy geraniums
• Hellebores • Hemerocallis • Violas

CHILLING SEEDS
Once the seeds are sown, water thoroughly, then plunge the pots in a sand bed outside, either in the open or in a cold frame, until they germinate.

Sow seed thinly

GOOD PLANTS FOR GROUND COVER

The descriptions here include symbols that summarize the plant's growing requirements. To calculate planting distances between different plants, halve the spread of each, add the two together, and then divide the total by two.

🔳 *Prefers full sun* 🔳 *Prefers partial shade* ▦ *Tolerates full shade* ◊ *Prefers well-drained soil* ◊ *Prefers moist soil* ◖ *Prefers wet soil* **H, S** *Approximate height and spread* ✳✳✳ *Fully hardy* ✳✳ *Frost hardy* ✳ *Half-hardy* ♀ *RHS Award of Garden Merit*

SHRUBS AND CLIMBERS

MOST OF THESE PLANTS are evergreen and make dense, weed-suppressing cover. Flowers or berries may add seasonal interest. Perennials (*see pp.70–77*) can be used as interplanting while they mature. Some are not fully hardy and suitable only for frost-free areas, or as seasonal planting in cold climates.

Arctostaphylos
Evergreen shrubs and small trees for acid soil. Low-growing *A. uva-ursi* makes useful ground cover; its tangled branches, only 10cm high, are covered with small oval leaves. Tiny pink flowers are produced in summer. *A. pumila* is similar but taller. H to 30cm S 50cm 🔳 ✳✳✳ ◊

Artemisia
Herbaceous or shrubby perennials that are often aromatic. The leaves may be green or silver, and evergreen or semi-evergreen. Prune in spring to keep compact. 🔳 ✳✳✳ ◊
Recommended: *A. ludoviciana* 'Silver Queen' ♀ H 75cm S 60 cm, *A. schmidtiana* ♀ H 30cm S 45cm.

Calluna vulgaris
(Heather, ling)
Low-growing, evergreen shrubs for acid soil with tiny leaves and white or purplish flowers in summer that attract bees.

ARCTOSTAPHYLOS PUMILA

H 30cm S 60cm 🔳 ✳✳✳ ◊
Recommended: 'Beoley Gold' ♀, 'Firefly' ♀, 'Red Star' ♀.

Ceanothus (Californian lilac)
Choose evergreen, sprawling types, with small glossy leaves on stiff branches that in late spring are covered with tiny, blue flowers. H 1m S 1.5m 🔳 ✳✳/✳✳✳ ◊ Recommended: *C. griseus* var. *horizontalis* 'Yankee Point', *C. thyrsiflorus* var. *repens* 'Ken Taylor' ♀.

Cistus (Rock rose, sun rose)
Aromatic, evergreen shrubs with showy but short-lived flowers in summer. Plants thrive in hot, dry soil. H 1m S 1.5m 🔳 ✳✳/✳✳✳ ◊ Recommended: *C.* × *corbariensis* ♀, *C.* × *dansereaui* 'Decumbens' ♀.

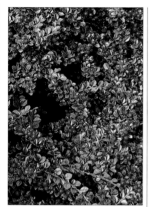

COTONEASTER HORIZONTALIS

Clematis
Usually grown as climbers, but can be used as ground cover if trained over a framework of horizontal branches or through shrubs such as conifers and cotoneasters.
H 60cm S 1.5m ◻ ✲✲✲ ◊
Recommended: 'Jackmanii' ♥, 'Minuet' ♥, C. tangutica.

Cotoneaster
Deciduous or evergreen shrubs with small white flowers in summer and red berries in autumn, providing cover and food for birds. Some make effective ground cover for slopes.
H 1m S 1.5m ◻ ◲ ✲✲✲ ◊
Recommended: 'Herbstfeuer', C. horizontalis ♥, C. procumbens, C. × suecicus 'Coral Beauty' and 'Skogholm'.

Daphne
Deciduous and evergreen shrubs usually grown for their sweetly-scented flowers. Some have a spreading habit.
H 75cm S 1m ✲✲✲ ◊
Recommended: D. cneorum 'Eximia' ♥ ◻, D. laureola ▩ ♥, D. pontica ♥ ◻.

Diervilla sessilifolia
Deciduous shrub spreading by suckers. The leaves are tinged with bronze in spring and the small, sulphur-yellow flowers open in summer.
H 1m S 1.5m ◻ ✲✲✲ ◊

Erica (Heather)
Evergreen shrubs of varied habit, with needle-like leaves on slender branches. The small, bell-shaped flowers are attractive to bees. Most need acid soil – only the winter-flowering sorts such as E. carnea and E. × darleyensis are lime-tolerant. All need an open, sunny site.
H 60cm S 1m ◻ ✲✲✲ ◊
Recommended: E. carnea, E. cinerea, E. × darleyensis, E. vagans.

Euonymus fortunei
(Spindle bush)
Small-leaved evergreen shrub, forming compact mounds in sun or shade. Leaves are brightly variegated but the plants have no floral beauty.
H 60cm S 2m ◻ ◲ ▣ ✲✲✲ ◊
Recommended: 'Emerald Gaiety' ♥, 'Emerald 'n' Gold' ♥.

DAPHNE LAUREOLA SUBSP. PHILIPPI

EUONYMUS FORTUNEI 'EMERALD 'N' GOLD'

Gaultheria
Vigorous, spreading evergreen shrubs for acid soil. Clusters of small pink or white flowers in spring are followed by red, pink or white berries.
H 60cm S 2m ◻ ◲ ✲✲✲ ◊
Recommended: G. shallon, G. mucronata 'Crimsonia' ♥ and 'Wintertime' ♥.

Genista
Small-leaved, often prickly shrubs with bright yellow flowers in summer. They are quick-growing and thrive on dry soils.
H 60cm S 1m ◻ ✲✲✲ ◊
Recommended:
G. hispanica ♥, G. lydia ♥.

Hebe
Evergreen shrubs with pairs of leaves set at right angles and clusters of small flowers. Some are rather tender, especially those with large leaves and flowers. Habit and form varies widely but all prefer well-drained soil.
H 45cm S 1m ◻ ✲✲/✲✲✲ ◊
Recommended: 'Autumn Glory', H. pinguifolia 'Pagei' ♥, H. rakaiensis ♥.

Hedera helix 'Luzii', 'Perkeo' and 'Goldchild'

Hedera helix (Ivy)
Evergreen climber that can be used for ground cover. Leaves come in a variety of sizes, shapes and colours. Thrives in shade and all soil types. The sap may irritate skin.
H 10cm S 1.5m ▣ ✳✳✳ ◊
Recommended: 'Buttercup' ♀ (best in sun for brightest-coloured leaves), 'Eva' ♀, 'Green Ripple', *H. hibernica* ♀, 'Manda's Crested' ♀.

Helianthemum (Sun rose)
Low-growing, evergreen shrubs with grey or green leaves and masses of small, bright flowers in summer. Useful for sunny positions and on dry banks.
H 20cm S 30cm ▣ ✳✳✳ ◊
Recommended: 'Fire Dragon' ♀, 'Henfield Brilliant' ♀, 'Rhodanthe Carneum' ♀, 'Wisley Primrose' ♀.

Hypericum calycinum
(Rose of Sharon)
Suckering low shrub with upright stems and evergreen leaves. Large golden flowers throughout summer.
H 20cm S 1m ▣ ✳✳✳ ◊

Iberis sempervirens
Dwarf evergreen shrub with deep green leaves. Pure white flowers in spring.
H 25cm S 60cm ▣ ✳✳✳ ◊
Recommended: 'Snowflake' ♀.

Lantana
Evergreen, tender shrubs for dry soil and warm climates. Domed clusters of small flowers are produced over a long season. The rough foliage that may cause skin irritation. Minimum 10°C.
H 75cm S 1.5m ▣ ◊
Recommended: *L. camara*, *L. montevidensis*.

Lantana camara

Lavandula (Lavender)
Grey-leaved, evergreen shrubs with aromatic foliage and spikes of fragrant flowers. If planted closely they make useful ground cover on dry soil and slopes.
H 45cm S 60cm ▣ ✳✳✳ ◊
Recommended:
L. angustifolia 'Hidcote' ♀, *L. × intermedia*.

Leucothoe walteri ♀
Evergreen shrub with attractive glossy foliage and clusters of small white flowers in spring. Young foliage is tinted red. Requires lime-free soil.
H 1m S 2m ▣ ✳✳✳ ◊
Recommended: 'Rainbow', 'Rollissonii' ♀.

Lotus berthelotii ♀
Low-growing evergreen with grey, needle-like leaves and showy scarlet flowers on older plants. Use as a bedding plant in cold climates. Minimum 10°C.
H 20cm S 2m ▣ ✳ ◊

Mahonia aquifolium
Evergreen with glossy, spiny leaves and fragrant, bright yellow flowers in winter or spring. Dark purple, edible berries ripen in autumn. It will self-seed in wild areas.
H 1m S 1.5m ▣ ✳✳✳ ◊
Recommended: *M. repens* 'Apollo' ♀, *M. × wagneri* 'Undulata' ♀.

Myrica cerifera
(Wax myrtle)
Mounded, suckering shrub for moist soil with aromatic leaves, tiny yellow flowers, and clusters of white fruits that last throughout winter.
H 5m S 5m ▣ ✳✳ ◊

LANTANA MONTEVIDENSIS

Nandina domestica ♀
(Heavenly bamboo)
Small, evergreen shrub with erect stems and finely-divided leaves, red-tinted when young and in winter. White flowers in summer and red berries.
H 1.5m S 1.5m ▣ ✳✳✳ ◊
Recommended: 'Firepower', 'Harbor Dwarf'.

Origanum (Marjoram)
Aromatic, dwarf shrubs and woody perennials with clusters of pink or purple flowers in summer. Useful in dry soils. Attractive to bees.
H 20cm S 60cm ▣ ✳✳✳ ◊
Recommended: O. *laevigatum* 'Herrenhausen' ♀, O. *vulgare* 'Aureum' ♀.

Parthenocissus
(Virginia creeper)
Deciduous climber with bright autumn colour. Useful as ground cover on slopes and banks where plants can extend over large areas. Excellent when underplanted with autumn-flowering colchicums.
H 20cm S 3m ▣ ✳✳✳ ◊
Recommended: P. *henryana*, P. *tricuspidata* ♀, 'Lowii' and 'Veitchii'.

SPREADING CONIFERS

Many dwarf or spreading conifers make excellent, low-maintenance, evergreen ground cover provided they are planted in full sun and moist but well-drained soil. When young, some conifers will withstand some treading, but as their branches become woody it is more difficult to walk through them without tripping or causing them damage, so restrict their use to areas that do not require regular access. All below are fully hardy.

Juniperus communis
Low-growing types such as 'Prostrata', 'Green Carpet' ♀ and 'Repanda' ♀ (H 30cm S 2m) make excellent cover on banks. They are very hardy, with fine foliage and blue or black fruits, and tolerate a range of soils, including chalk.

Juniperus conferta
Naturally low-growing, with pointed green leaves and a spreading habit. H 30cm S 2m.
Recommended: 'Blue Ice', 'Blue Pacific'.

Juniperus horizontalis
Creeping, with greyish, sharply pointed, needle-like leaves. Dark blue fruits.
H 30cm S 2m.
Recommended: 'Bar Harbor', 'Blue Chip', 'Emerald Spreader', 'Grey Pearl', 'Plumosa' ♀, 'Turquoise Spreader', 'Wiltonii' ♀.

Juniperus sabina
Spreading, with reddish bark. The foliage smells unpleasant if crushed. H 60cm S 2m.
Recommended: 'Blaue Donau', 'Cupressifolia', 'Skandia'.

Juniperus squamata
Low-growing types such as 'Blue Carpet' ♀ and 'Holger' ♀ are useful ground cover in most soils. Spiny leaves in shades of grey-green.
H 40cm–1m S 1–2m.

Microbiota decussata ♀
Low-growing, with sprays of tiny, triangular leaves that turn bronze in winter.
H 1m S 2m or more.

Picea abies
Low-growing Norway spruces such as 'Inversa' and 'Reflexa' (H 15cm S 2m or more) are suitable as ground cover. Dark green needles.

Thuja occidentalis
Eventually, this is a small, conical tree, but there are dwarf white cedars that can be planted to make interesting, dense ground cover, though none is strictly prostrate.
Recommended: 'Caespitosa', 'Golden Globe'.

Thujopsis dolobrata
A conical tree with white undersides to the leaves. 'Nana' (H 1m S80cm) can be used for ground cover.

THUJA OCCIDENTALIS 'CAESPITOSA'

ROSMARINUS OFFICINALIS
PROSTRATUS GROUP

Paxistima canbyi

Spreading evergreen shrub
with small, leathery leaves
and hanging clusters of
insignificant greenish flowers
in summer.
H 40cm S 1m ◘ ✳✳✳ ◊

Rhus aromatica

Prostrate shrub with divided
foliage that often colours well
before falling. Yellow flower
spikes. May sucker freely and
can become a nuisance. Wear
gloves when handling: most
Rhus have irritant sap that
may cause skin blisters.
H 1.5m S 3m ◘ ✳✳✳ ◊

Rosmarinus officinalis

Evergreen shrub with narrow,
aromatic leaves and pale blue
flowers in spring and early
summer. Thrives in dry, poor
soil and is excellent for dry
banks. Except for the
prostrate forms listed below,
rosemaries make upright
plants at first, becoming
spreading with age.
H 1.5m S 1.5m ◘ ✳✳/✳✳✳ ◊
Recommended: 'Jackman's
Prostrate', Prostratus Group ♡,
'Severn Sea'.

Rubus

Evergreen and deciduous
shrubs with varying habits.
The best for ground cover are
the creeping species below,
which are useful in shade and
can spread over large areas,
though they may swamp
delicate plants.
H 60cm S 3m ▓ ✳✳✳ ◊
Recommended: *R. pentalobus*,
R. tricolor.

Ruscus

Spreading evergreen with
woody stems. Tiny flowers
are followed by red berries on
female plants. Slowly forms
dense clumps and is never
invasive. Will tolerate dense
shade and dry soil, but thrives
in better conditions.
H 75cm S 1m ▓ ✳✳✳ ◊
Recommended: *R. aculeatus*,
R. hypoglossum.

Salix repens

Low-growing, deciduous
willow with grey-green leaves,
and golden catkins in spring,
before the leaves unfold on
the slender branches.
H 60cm S 2m ◘ ✳✳✳ ◊
Recommended: *S. repens*; var.
argentea (for silky grey leaves).

SALIX REPENS

SARCOCOCCA RUSCIFOLIA

Santolina

Dwarf, evergreen shrubs with
aromatic foliage that may be
green or grey. Small, globular
flowerheads are produced in
summer. Pruning in spring
will keep plants compact and
extend their life.
H 50cm S 1m ◘ ✳✳✳ ◊
Recommended:
S. chamaecyparissus ♡,
S. pinnata subsp. *neapolitana*
♡, *S. rosmarinifolia* 'Primrose
Gem' ♡.

Sarcococca

(Sweet box, Christmas box)
Evergreen, suckering shrubs
with small glossy leaves. Will
form dense clumps. Tiny,
white, fragrant flowers in late
winter are followed by red or
black berries.
H 1.2m S 1.2m ▓ ✳✳✳ ◊
Recommended: *S. ruscifolia*
var. *chinensis* ♡, *S. confusa* ♡,
S. hookeriana ♡.

Stephandra incisa

Small, suckering, arching
shrub with inconspicuous
flowers but bright autumn
colour. Thrives in sun or
partial shade in most soils.
H 1m S 2m ◘ ✳✳✳ ◊

VINCA MINOR

Thymus (Thyme)
Creeping evergreen shrub
with tiny aromatic leaves and
clusters of small flowers in
summer. Tolerates poor soil
and light treading but watch
for bees when in flower.
H 20cm S 50cm ▣ ✳✳✳ ◊
Recommended: *T. doerfleri*
'Bressingham', *T.* 'Doone
Valley', *T. serpyllum
coccineus* ♀, *T. serpyllum*
'Pink Chintz' ♀.

Trachelospermum
Twining evergreen climber
with glossy leaves and white,
starry, fragrant flowers in
summer. Can be used as
ground cover in mild climates
in sun or partial shade.
H 20cm S 5m ▣ ✳✳ ◊
Recommended:
T. jasminoides ♀,
T. jasminoides 'Variegatum' ♀.

Vaccinium vitis-idaea
(Cranberry)
Creeping evergreen shrub
with white or pink flowers
in spring, followed by red
berries. Requires acid soil.
H 25cm S 1m ▣ ✳✳✳ ◊
Recommended: Koralle
Group ♀.

Vinca (Periwinkle)
Creeping evergreens with
arching shoots that root when
they touch the soil. They
tolerate poor and damp soil
and deep shade. Blue, pink or
white flowers in spring and
into summer. Useful on banks
and rough areas; use *V. major*
only where there is plenty of
room. H 30cm S 1m ▣ ✳✳✳ ◊
Recommended: *V. major*
'Maculata' and 'Variegata' ♀,
V. minor 'Argenteovariegata'
♀, 'Atropurpurea' ♀ and
'La Grave' ♀.

Vitis coignetiae
Vigorous climber with
large leaves that take on
spectacular autumn shades.
Useful for covering a sunny
bank where there is room.
H 50cm S 5m ▣ ✳✳✳ ◊

**Xanthorrhiza
simplicissima**
Suckering, deciduous shrub
with ferny leaves. Pendent,
brownish flowers in spring
but the main attraction is
the bright autumn colour.
H 60cm S 2m ▣ ✳✳✳ ◊

GROUND-COVER ROSES

The range of ground-cover
roses is ever-increasing. Some
are small, dense, bushy plants;
others have creeping, trailing
stems that may root where
they touch the ground. They
are dull in winter, when they
have lost their leaves, but most
are swathed in a succession of
blooms from late spring through
the summer. They are resistant
to diseases and need minimal
pruning (*see p.60*). ▣ ✳✳✳ ◊

ROSA 'SURREY'

'Broadlands' Vigorous, with
double creamy-yellow flowers.
H 75cm S 1.3m.

Grouse Trailing, with single,
scented, pale pink flowers.
H 60cm S 3m.

'Nozomi' ♀ Trailing, with
clusters of single, pale pink
flowers. H 45cm S 1.5m.

Pink Bells Vigorous, with
deep pink flowers. H 75cm
S 1.5m.

Surrey ♀ Mound-forming,
with double pink flowers.
H 80cm S 1.2m.

Swany Trailing, with double
white flowers. H 75cm S 1.5m.

Snow Carpet ♀ Miniature
with cream flowers. H. 15cm
S 50cm.

The Fairy ♀ Cushion-forming,
with double pink blooms.
H 75cm S 1m.

ROSA GROUSE

PERENNIALS

THESE PLANTS OFTEN COVER the ground more quickly than shrubs, but need more maintenance. In winter, stems may need cutting down, and a mulch of organic matter and a feed in spring will ensure vigorous growth. Use the given spread as a planting distance and divide plants as they grow and fill the gaps between.

Achillea (Yarrow)
Mat-forming or upright perennials, usually with small flowers in flat heads. Low-growing species are listed below. Leaves may be grey or green and often finely-divided. Suitable for dry soils in sun.
H 2.5m S 3m ◪ ✱✱✱ ◊
Recommended: *A. ageratum* 'W. B. Childs', *A. ptarmica* 'Boule de Neige' and 'Schwellenburg', *A. tomentosa* ♛.

Aegopodium podagraria 'Variegata'
Variegated version of ground elder, the invasive weed that can thrive in even the most adverse conditions. Useful bright cover in rough areas of ground but plant only where it cannot swamp other plants.
H 30 cm S 3m ◪ ✱✱✱ ◊

AJUGA REPTANS 'MULTICOLOR'

Agapanthus (African lily)
Clump-forming perennials with strap-shaped leaves. Deciduous species are more frost hardy than evergreens. Rounded heads of blue flowers on tall stems in summer.
H 1.2m S 1m ◪ ✱✱ ◊
Recommended: *A. africanus* ♛, *A. campanulatus*, Headbourne Hybrids, 'Lilliput', 'Loch Hope' ♛.

Ajuga reptans
Creeping, semi-evergreen perennial with glossy leaves, which can be red or purplish, or even multi-coloured, and short spikes of, usually, blue flowers in early summer.
H 15cm S 60cm ◪ ✱✱✱ ◊
Recommended: 'Atropurpurea' ♛, 'Braunherz' ♛, 'Burgundy Glow' ♛, 'Catlin's Giant' ♛, 'Multicolor'.

Alchemilla (Lady's mantle)
Woody-based perennials with rounded leaves and sprays of small, yellowish-green flowers in summer.
H 45cm S 60cm ◪ ✱✱✱ ◊
Recommended: *A. alpina*, *A. mollis* ♛.

Anthemis punctata subsp. **cupaniana** ♛
Clump-forming or spreading, with white, yellow-centred daisy flowers in summer above fine, silver foliage.
H 30cm S 75cm ◪ ✱✱✱ ◊

ALCHEMILLA MOLLIS

Arabis (Rock cress)
Evergreen, cushion-forming perennial with dull green leaves and massed white or pink flowers in spring. Useful on dry and chalky soils and on banks.
H 15cm S 50cm ◪ ✱✱✱ ◊
Recommended: *A. alpina* 'Flore Pleno' ♛ and 'Snowcap' ♛, *A. blepharophylla* 'Frühlingszauber' ♛.

Asarum (Wild ginger)
Evergreen perennials with glossy, dark green, aromatic foliage and curious brown flowers that lie hidden at soil level. Grows best in lime-free soil where plants form dense, low mats of leaves.
H 8cm S 45cm ◪ ✱✱✱ ◊
Recommended: *A. europaeum*, *A. shuttleworthii*.

Bergenia (Elephant's ears)
Spring-flowering perennial
with pink or white blooms
and bold, glossy, rounded
evergreen leaves that often
assume red and burgundy
tints in winter. Adaptable to
most soils and conditions.
H 30cm S 60cm ▣ ✳✳✳ ◊
Recommended: 'Bressingham
White' ♀, *B. cordifolia*
'Purpurea' ♀, 'Morgenröte' ♀,
B. purpurascens ♀,
'Silberlicht' ♀.

Brunnera macrophylla ♀
Clump-forming perennial
with bold, heart-shaped
leaves, sometimes variegated,
and sprays of small, blue
flowers in late spring.
H 45cm S 60cm ▣ ✳✳✳ ◊
Recommended: 'Langtrees',
'Hadspen Cream' ♀.

Campanula (Bell flower)
Widely varying perennials,
most with blue, bell-shaped
flowers. Low-growing species
make vigorous cover.
H 15cm S 50cm ▣ ✳✳✳ ◊
Recommended: *C. garganica* ♀,
C. portenschlagiana ♀,
C. porscharskyana.

ANTHEMIS PUNCTATA SUBSP.
CUPANIANA

CAMPANULA PORSCHARSKYANA

Cerastium tomentosum
(Snow-in-summer)
Rampant, mat-forming
perennial with silver leaves
and white flowers in summer.
Useful in dry soil and rough
areas and on banks, but it can
be invasive in borders.
H 10 cm S 1m ▣ ✳✳✳ ◊

Ceratostigma
Semi-shrubby or herbaceous
perennials with bright blue
flowers in autumn, set against
leaves that turn red. Valuable
for its late flowers.
H 45cm S 1m ▣ ✳✳✳ ◊
Recommended:
C. plumbaginoides ♀,
C. willmottianum ♀.

Chamaemelum nobile
(Camomile)
Mat-forming, aromatic
perennial with finely-divided
leaves and white daisy flowers
in summer. Often used as a
lawn because it withstands
light treading, and is
commonly mixed with
thymes, though it is difficult
to produce a formal effect.
Requires "mowing" unless
'Treneague' is planted.
H 30cm S 45cm ▣ ✳✳✳ ◊

Convallaria majalis ♀
(Lily-of-the-valley)
Creeping perennial with
broad, basal leaves and spikes
of fragrant, pendent, bell-
shaped, white, occasionally
pink, flowers in late spring.
Prefers moist soil and semi-
shade, where it can be invasive.
H 23cm S 30cm ▣ ✳✳✳ ◊
Recommended: 'Fortin's
Giant', var. *rosea*.

Convolvulus
Shrubs, annuals, or scrambling
perennials with attractive
funnel-shaped flowers,
twining stems, and often
invasive roots (bindweed is a
relation). Those suitable for
ground cover prefer well-
drained soil and sun and are
less hardy in rich, moist soil.
H 15cm S 1m
Recommended: *C. althaeoides*
▣ ✳✳✳ ◊, *C. sabatius* ♀ ✳✳ ◊.

Cotula coronopifolia
Moisture-loving, short-lived
perennial that will self-seed.
Coarsely-toothed leaves and
bright yellow, button-like
flowers in summer.
H 15cm S 30cm ▣ ✳✳✳ ◊

CONVALLARIA MAJALIS

Dicentra (Bleeding heart)
Spreading perennials with
divided leaves and arching
stems with pendent, heart-
shaped flowers, usually in
shades of pink or white. For
partial shade and moist soil;
dies back in drought or sun.
H 45cm S 60cm ◩ ✳✳✳ ◊
Recommended: 'Bacchanal',
'Langtrees' ♀, 'Luxuriant' ♀,
'Stuart Boothman' ♀.

Duchesnea indica
Creeping plant that spreads
by runners. Resembles a
strawberry. Yellow flowers
are followed by red, edible
but insipid fruit.
H 10cm S 1.2m ◩ ✳✳✳ ◊
Recommended: 'Harlequin'.

Epimedium (Barrenwort)
Rhizomatous, semi-evergreen
or evergreen perennials with
delicate, colourful flowers in
spring. To show off the
flowers, trim away old foliage
in winter. Plants thrive in
moist soils, but some tolerate
dry shade when established.
H 40cm S 60cm ◩ ✳✳✳ ◊
Recommended:
E. grandiflorum 'Rose Queen'
♀, E. × perralchicum ♀.

EPIMEDIUM × PERRALCHICUM

GERANIUM ENDRESSII

Euphorbia (Spurge)
Diverse group of plants for all
climates. Many frost-hardy
species are suitable for ground
cover. Most have flowers with
showy bracts, usually in
shades of yellow or green.
H 45cm S 60cm ✳✳✳ ◊
Recommended: E.
amygdaloides var. robbiae ♀ ▣ ,
E. cyparissias 'Fens Ruby' ◧,
E. dulcis 'Chameleon' ◧,
E. griffithii 'Dixter' ♀ ◧,
E. polychroma ♀ ◧.

Galium odoratum
(Sweet woodruff)
Spreading, aromatic perennial
with small, whorled leaves
and tiny, white, scented
flowers. Tolerates poor soil.
H 45cm S 1.2m ◧ ✳✳✳ ◊

Geranium
Summer-flowering perennials,
many with a spreading habit.
Foliage is often greyish or
attractively marked. Flowers
come in shades of pink, blue,
purple, and white.
H 40cm S 60cm ◩ ✳✳✳ ◊
Recommended: G. endressii
♀, 'Johnson's Blue' ♀,
G. macrorrhizum 'Album' ♀,
G. × oxonianum.

Helleborus (Hellebore)
Winter- and early-spring
flowering, evergreen
perennials that form clumps
of deep green leaves. They
provide permanent ground
cover if planted closely. Some
thrive in deep shade, once
established, and also on
chalky soil. They spread by
self-sown seedlings.
H 45cm S 60cm ◩ ✳✳✳ ◊
Recommended:
H. argutifolius, H. foetidus
Wester Flisk Group,
H. orientalis.

Hemerocallis (Daylily)
Clump-forming perennials
with long, narrow leaves and
large, funnel-shaped flowers
in summer. Habit and vigour
vary and dwarf types are
useful for edging and ground
cover. Some spread quickly by
underground shoots. Most
thrive in moist soil but
flower most freely when
grown in full sun. Each
flower lasts only one day, but
they are produced over a long
period. Orange, yellow and
pink are the most common
flower colours.
H 70cm S 1m ◧ ✳✳✳ ◊

HEUCHERA 'RED SPANGLES'

Heuchera

Evergreen and semi-evergreen
perennials with attractive
leaves and spikes of small,
often brightly-coloured
flowers. Those with coloured
leaves are especially useful for
ground cover.
H 60cm S 45cm ▧ ✳✳✳ ◊
Recommended: 'Chocolate
Ruffles', *H. micrantha* 'Palace
Purple' ♥, 'Persian Carpet',
'Red Spangles' ♥.

Hosta

Clump-forming or
rhizomatous perennials with
bold foliage, often glaucous
or variegated, and spikes of
pendent, funnel-shaped
flowers in shades of white
and purple in mid-summer.
Most prefer moist soil in part
shade, but many are drought-
resistant when established.
The following include those
that will thrive in most
conditions.
H to 75cm S 1m ▧ ✳✳✳ ◊
Recommended: White-
variegated: *H. fortunei* var.
albopicta ♥, 'Francee' ♥,
'Wide Brim' ♥; Blue-leaved:
'Krossa Regal' ♥,
H. sieboldiana var. *elegans*,
'Shade Fanfare' ♥; Yellow-
variegated: *H. fortunei* var.
aureomarginata ♥, 'Frances
Williams' ♥, 'Gold Standard',
'Sum and Substance' ♥.

Houttuynia cordata

Rhizomatous, deciduous
perennial with reddish stems
of heart-shaped leaves and
small white flowers. Leaves
have a pungent scent when
crushed. Can be invasive in
moist soil.
H 30cm S 1m ▧ ✳✳✳ ◊ ◉
Recommended: 'Chameleon',
'Flame'.

HOSTA SIEBOLDIANA
VAR. ELEGANS

Lamium (Dead nettle)

Creeping, evergreen or semi-
evergreen perennials with
whorls of small flowers in
early summer. Square stems
with opposite leaves, often
attractively marked. Some
lamiums may be invasive, but
they are useful in dry shade.
H 30cm S 1m ▧ ✳✳✳ ◊
Recommended:
L. galeobdolon, *L. galeobdolon*
'Hermann's Pride' and 'Silver
Carpet', *L. maculatum*
'Beacon Silver' and 'White
Nancy' ♥, *L. orvala*.

Lampranthus

Succulent, shrubby perennials
for mild gardens. In cold
areas use as summer bedding.
In summer, plants produce
bright, daisy-like flowers.
Useful in arid, frost-free
climates. Minimum 7°C.
H 45cm S 1m ▧ ◊
Recommended:
L. aurantiacus, *L. spectabilis*
'Tresco Apricot'.

Liriope (Lilyturf)

Clump-forming, evergreen
perennial with narrow, grassy
leaves and spikes of tiny

HOSTA 'GOLD STANDARD'

mauve or white flowers in
autumn. Prefers acid soil but
is tolerant of drought and
some shade.
H 30cm S 45cm ▧ ✳✳✳ ◊
Recommended: *L. muscari*,
L. muscari 'Variegata'.

Luzula (Woodrush)

Evergreen, tufted, grass-like
perennials with small, dull
flowers, often in attractive
heads. Useful in poor but
moist soil.
H 75cm S 60cm ▧ ✳✳✳ ◊
Recommended: *L. nivea*,
L. sylvatica 'Aurea' and
'Marginata'.

LUZULA NIVEA

NEPETA × FAASSENII

Lysimachia (Loosestrife)
Usually deciduous, spreading
perennials with upright stems
and spikes of small flowers,
though Creeping Jenny,
L. nummularia, is low and
prostrate. Most prefer fairly
moist soil.
H 75cm S 60cm ▣ ✳✳✳ ♦
Recommended: *L. clethroides*
♥, *L. nummularia* 'Aurea' ♥,
L. punctata 'Alexander'.

Mazus reptans
Creeping, small-leaved
perennial with mauve flowers.
Prefers moist but well-drained
soil and thrives in peat beds.
H 5cm S 30cm ▣ ✳✳ ♦

Mentha (Mint)
Creeping, deciduous
perennials that may be
invasive. Low-growing species
make useful, fragrant ground
cover, with flowers that are
attractive to bees.
H 45cm S 1m ▣ ✳✳✳ ♦
Recommended: *M.* × *gracilis*
'Variegata', *M. pulegium, M.
requienii, M. spicata* 'Crispa',
M. suaveolens 'Variegata'.

Nepeta (Catmint)
Aromatic perennials, often
with greyish leaves and blue
flowers. Habit varies from
upright to trailing. Plants
thrive in dry soils and the
flowers in summer attract bees.
H 45cm S 60cm ▣ ✳✳✳ ♦
Recommended: *N.* × *faassenii,*
N. racemosa, N. sibirica
'Souvenir d'André Chaudron',
N. 'Six Hills Giant'.

Ophiopogon
Rhizomatous evergreens with
green, black or variegated
grass-like leaves. The small,
flowers on short spikes are
followed by round fruits.
H 25cm S 30cm ▣ ✳✳✳ ♦
Recommended: *O. jaburan*
'Vittatus', *O. planiscapus*
'Nigrescens' ♥.

Osteospermum
Slightly frost-tender, evergreen
perennials with daisy-like
flowers throughout summer.
Habits vary, but low-growing
species make good ground
cover in sun on light soils in
sheltered places.
H 30cm S 75cm ▣ ✳✳ ♦
Recommended: 'Cannington
Roy', *O. jucundum* ♥,
'Nairobi Purple'.

Pachysandra terminalis ♥
Spreading evergreen with
glossy leaves and small
clusters of insignificant white
flowers in early summer.
Flourishes in moist, acidic soil
in shade.
H 15cm S 60cm ▣ ✳✳✳ ♦
Recommended: 'Green
Carpet', 'Variegata' ♥.

Persicaria
Evergreen or deciduous
perennials of bushy or
creeping habit. The poker-like
flowerheads in shades of pink
are produced in profusion
over a long period in summer.
H 75cm S 1m ▣ ✳✳✳ ♦
Recommended: *P. affinis*
'Darjeeling Red' ♥,
P. amplexicaulis 'Firetail' ♥,
P. campanulata 'Rosenrot'.

RECOMMENDED HARDY FERNS

In moist soils, in shade, ferns
make elegant ground cover.

Blechnum penna-marina
A glossy evergreen that spreads
widely. Needs acid soil.
H 20cm S 1m

Dryopteris erythrosora ♥
Slowly creeping, with finely
divided fronds that are copper-
red when young.
H 60cm S 40cm

Matteuccia struthiopteris ♥
Fronds arranged in narrow
"shuttlecocks". H 1.2m S 1m

Onoclea sensibilis ♥
Deciduous, with deeply-
divided fronds, tinted pink in
spring. H 60cm S 1m

Polypodium vulgare
'Cornubiense' Vigorous;
divided evergreen fronds.
H 30cm S 80cm

BLECHNUM PENNA-MARINA

PACHYSANDRA TERMINALIS

Potentilla (Cinquefoil)
Clump-forming perennials with divided leaves and showy five-petalled flowers in summer. Most thrive in poor, dry soils in sun. Wide variation in plant habit.
H 45cm S 45cm ❑ ✳✳✳ ◊
Recommended: *P. alba*, *P. aurea*, *P. eriocarpa*, *P. nepalensis* 'Miss Willmott'.

Pratia
Low, creeping evergreen with tiny leaves and starry blue or white flowers in summer. Can spread rapidly in moist soil in sun and will grow in lawns.
H 5cm S 60cm ❑ ✳✳✳ ◊
Recommended: *P. angulata* 'Treadwellii', *P. pedunculata*, *P. pedunculata* 'County Park'.

Prunella grandiflora
(Self-heal)
Low, spreading, semi-evergreen with a woody base. The dense spikes of pink, white or purple flowers open throughout summer. Related to the lawn weed but far superior in appearance.
H 15cm S 1m ❑ ✳✳✳ ◊
Recommended: 'Loveliness' ♀, 'Pink Loveliness'.

Pulmonaria (Lungwort)
A deciduous or evergreen woodland plant with pink, blue, or white flowers in early spring. These are followed by leaves that are often marked with silver. It prefers moist soil and part shade, and is prone to mildew in dry soil.
H 25cm S 45cm ❑ ✳✳✳ ◊
Recommended: *P. angustifolia* ♀, 'Lewis Palmer' ♀, *P. officinalis* 'Sissinghurst White' ♀, *P. rubra* ♀, *P. saccharata* Argentea Group ♀.

Sagina subulata
Low-growing, moss-like plant with narrow leaves and small white flowers on short stems. Useful as cover in shady areas and between paving.
H 1cm S 30cm ❑ ✳✳✳ ◊
Recommended: 'Aurea'.

Sanguinaria canadensis
(Bloodroot)
Rhizomatous woodland perennial with lobed, round, glaucous leaves and white, fleeting flowers in spring. The double-flowered 'Plena' has longer-lasting blooms.
H 15cm S 30cm ❑ ✳✳✳ ◊
Recommended: 'Plena' ♀.

PERSICARIA AFFINIS 'SUPERBA'

PULMONARIA SACCHARATA

Saxifraga
Alpine and woodland plants with rosettes of attractive foliage and sprays of small, five-petalled flowers, usually in spring.
H 25cm S 30cm ❑ ✳✳✳ ◊
Recommended: 'Cloth of Gold', *S. stolonifera* ♀, *S. umbrosa* var. *primuloides* ♀, *S.* × *urbium* ♀ (London pride).

Sedum
Succulent, sun-loving plants with clusters of small, starry flowers that attract bees.
H 30cm S 45cm ❑ ✳✳✳ ◊
Recommended: *S. acre* 'Aureum', 'Autumn Joy' ♀, *S. kamschaticum* 'Variegatum' ♀, *S. spathulifolium* 'Purpureum' ♀, *S. spurium* 'Dragon's Blood' ♀.

Sempervivum
Succulent plants that spread to form mats of rosettes; these can vary in size and colour. Will survive in arid conditions and very poor soil.
H 20cm S 30cm ❑ ✳✳✳ ◊
Recommended: *S. arachnoideum* ♀, 'Commander Hay' ♀, *S. tectorum* ♀.

Soleirolia soleirolii
(Mind-your-own-business)
Creeping evergreen with tiny
leaves and insignificant
flowers. Will cover both soil
and rocks in moist conditions
in mild climates, and can
become invasive.
H 10cm S 1m ▣ ✳✳ ◊
Recommended: 'Aurea',
'Variegata'.

Stachys
Clump-forming or creeping
plants, often with grey, velvety
leaves, for sun or part shade.
Spikes of purplish flowers in
summer may be showy but
are best removed as they fade.
H 30cm S 60cm ▣ ✳✳✳ ◊
Recommended: *S. byzantina*
'Big Ears' and 'Silver Carpet',
S. macrantha 'Robusta' ♀.

Symphytum (Comfrey)
Coarse-leaved perennials with
branched stems of drooping,
tubular flowers in summer.
Spreading or clump-forming.
H 60cm S 60cm ▣ ✳✳✳ ◊
Recommended:
S. caucasicum, *S.* 'Goldsmith'
♀, *S.* × *uplandicum*
'Variegatum' ♀.

*SYMPHYTUM
CAUCASICUM*

STACHYS BYZANTINA

Tanacetum
Diverse annuals and
perennials with usually white
or yellow daisy flowers, and
often with attractive, divided
foliage. Most prefer light, dry
soils and full sun. Feverfew
(*T. parthenium*) self-seeds
prolifically to form ground
cover on bare soil. Others
have grey foliage, which is
their main attraction.
H 30cm S 45cm ▣ ✳✳✳ ◊
Recommended: *T. argenteum*,
T. densum subsp. *amani*,
T. parthenium 'Aureum'.

Tellima grandiflora
Clump-forming perennial
with rosettes of kidney-shaped
leaves, sometimes tinged red
or purple. The tall spikes
of bell-shaped, greenish
flowers are produced in early
summer. Thrives in partial
shade in moist soil but is
also drought tolerant.
A suitable plant for woodland
gardens and as semi-evergreen
ground cover under shrubs in
most soils.
H 75cm S 30cm ▣ ✳✳✳ ◊
Recommended:
'Purpurteppich' ('Purple
Carpet'), Rubra Group.

Tiarella (Foam flower)
Woodland plants that form
spreading carpets of leaves
with spikes of small fluffy
flowers in summer. Those of
T. cordifolia ♀ are white; on
T. wherryi ♀ they are often
flushed with pink.
H 20cm S 30cm ▣ ✳✳✳ ◊

Tolmiea menziesii
(Pick-a-back plant)
Fast-spreading semi-evergreen
with kidney-shaped, lobed
leaves. Slender spikes of small
brownish flowers appear in
early summer. A fascinating
plant in that it produces new
plants on its leaves that root
as they touch the soil.
H 45cm S 60cm ▣ ✳✳✳ ◊
Recommended: 'Taff's Gold' ♀.

Trachystemon orientalis
Vigorous spreader with star-
shaped blue flowers in spring
before the coarse, heart-
shaped, bright green leaves.
Thrives in rough woodland,
that is not too dry, where it
forms dense colonies that
smother weeds and tolerate
summer drought.
H 30cm S 1m ▣ ✳✳✳ ◊ ◊

TELLIMA GRANDIFLORA
RUBRA GROUP

Tradescantia

Creeping or clump-forming plants with narrow leaves and three-petalled flowers. The creeping species are not frost hardy but in mild climates form excellent, rampant ground cover. Frost-hardy, clump-forming species are effective if planted closely. H 45cm S 60cm ◪ ◊
Recommended: *T.* × *andersoniana* 'Isis' ♀ ✻✻✻ and 'Osprey' ♀ ✻✻✻, *T. fluminensis* 'Quicksilver' ♀ ✻, *T. sillamontana* ♀ ✻.

TIARELLA WHERRYI

Viola (Violet)

Clump-forming plants with attractive, often scented, violet, white or yellow flowers in spring and summer. Some self-seed to form effective ground cover.
H 15cm S 30cm ◪ ✻✻✻ ◊
Recommended: *V. cornuta* ♀, *V. hederacea* ✻✻, *V. odorata*, *V. riviniana* Purpurea Group.

Waldsteinia ternata

Creeping, semi-evergreen plant with bright yellow, strawberry-like flowers in spring. Can cover large areas.
H 10cm S 60cm ▣ ✻✻✻ ◊

BULBS

Plant bulbs among ground-cover perennials and shrubs to brighten bare earth or green carpets of leaves in spring, or to contrast with coloured foliage or other kinds of flowers.

Ensure flowering heights are taller than the carpeting plants. Most bulbs are tolerant of lime in the soil and withstand summer drought, though they need moisture in spring when in growth. Few thrive in the dense shade of evergreens but are happy under deciduous shrubs. All the plants listed here are hardy.

Allium

Round heads of starry flowers in summer. H to 45cm ◪
Recommended: *A. cristophii* ♀, *A. hollandicum* ♀, *A. karataviense* ♀.

Chionodoxa

Early-spring flowers in shades of blue, or pink, usually with a white centre. H 15cm ◪
Recommended: *C. forbesii* Siehei Group ♀, *C. sardensis* ♀.

Colchicum

Mauve, goblet-shaped blooms in autumn and large leaves in spring. H 20cm ◪
Recommended: *C. speciosum* 'Album' ♀.

NARCISSUS CYCLAMINEUS

GALANTHUS 'FLORE PLENO'

Erythronium

(Dog's tooth violet)
Woodland bulbs with pretty flowers with reflexed petals in spring and early summer and marbled leaves. H 20cm ◪
Recommended: *E. dens-canis* ♀, 'Pagoda' ♀.

Galanthus (Snowdrop)

Delightful white flowers in late winter and early spring. Easy to grow. H 15cm ◪
Recommended: *G. elwesii* ♀ *G. nivalis* 'Flore Pleno' ♀.

Leucojum (Snowflake)

Leafy bulbs with white, bell-shaped flowers in spring and early summer. H 20cm ◪
Recommended: *L. aestivum* 'Gravetye Giant' ♀, *L. vernum* ♀.

Narcissus (Daffodil)

Spring-flowering bulbs, with flowers in shades of white and yellow. H to 40cm ◪
Recommended: 'Actaea' ♀, *N. cyclamineus* ♀, 'February Gold' ♀, 'Ice Follies' ♀, 'Tête-à-tête' ♀.

Scilla (Squill)

Mostly spring-flowering, with blue, sometimes pink or white flowers. H 15cm ◪ ◪
Recommended: *S. siberica* ♀.

INDEX

ACKNOWLEDGMENTS

Picture research Sean Hunter

Illustrations Karen Cochrane

Index Ella Skene

Dorling Kindersley would like to thank:
All staff at the RHS, in particular Susanne
Mitchell, Karen Wilson and Barbara Haynes
at Vincent Square; Lesley Malkin for editorial
assistance.

The Royal Horticultural Society
To learn more about the work of the Society,
visit the RHS on the internet at
www.rhs.org.uk. Information includes news
of events around the country, a horticultural
database, international plant registers, results
of plant trials and membership details.

Photography
The publisher would also like to thank the
following for their kind permission to
reproduce their photographs:
(key: t=top, c=centre, b=below, l=left, r=right)

Garden Picture Library: Brian Carter 14br,
56bl, 56bc; Brigitte Thomas 8tr, 13br;
Christopher Gallagher 50tr; Eric Crichton 55bl;
Howard Rice 33tl; Jacqui Hurst 23clb; Jane
Legate 23crb, 40cl; John Glover 10br, 42crb,
45tr; JS Sira 33tr; Mayer/Le Scanff 9tl, 49br;
Ron Sutherland 54. **John Glover:** 8b, 10bl,
15t, 44cra, 51bl. **Jerry Harpur:** 6, 11t, 14t,
34tr, 49tl. **Holt Studios International:** 41cl,
42bc, 42cra. **Andrew Lawson:** 9tr, 23tc,
25crb, 28crb, 33br, 45br, 57cl. **Clive Nichols:**
4bl, 23tr, Greystone Cottage, Oxon. 24cl,
48cl, Hilary Macpherson 12, Vale End, Surrey
22crb. **Harry Smith Collection:** 38cl, 39tl, 40br.

Jacket: **Garden Picture Library:** Brigitte Thomas
back tl. **John Glover:** front cla, front c, back c.
Andrew Lawson: front bl, front bla, back tr.